MOSES

MOSES

Gerhard von Rad

Translated by Stephen Neill

Foreword by Walter Brueggemann

Edited by K. C. Hanson

CASCADE *Books* · Eugene, Oregon

MOSES
Second edition

Copyright © 2011 James Clarke & Co. Foreword copyright © 2011 Walter
Brueggemann. All rights reserved. Except for brief quotations in critical
publications or reviews, no part of this book may be reproduced in any manner
without prior written permission from the publisher. Write: Permissions, Wipf
and Stock Publishers, 199 W. 8th Ave., Suite 3, Eugene, OR 97401.

Published by arrangment with James Clarke & Co.

Cascade Books
A Division of Wipf and Stock Publishers
199 W. 8th Ave., Suite 3
Eugene, OR 97401

www.wipfandstock.com

ISBN 13: 978-1-60608-771-8

Cataloging-in-Publication data:

    Rad, Gerhard von, 1901–1970.

    Moses / Gerhard von Rad ; translated by Stephen Neill ; edited with new
notes and bibliography by K. C. Hanson ; foreword by Walter Brueggemann —
2nd edition.

    ISBN 13: 978-1-60608-771-8

    xiv + 98 p. ; 21 cm. Includes bibliographical references and indexes.

    First English edition, Lutterworth, 1960.

    1. Moses (Biblical leader). 2. Bible. O.T. Pentateuch. 3. Rad, Gerhard von,
1901–1970. I. Neill, Stephen, 1900–1984. II. Hanson, K. C. (Kenneth Charles).
III. Brueggemann, Walter. IV. Title.

BS580 M6 R23 2011

Manufactured in the U.S.A.

Scripture quotations are from the New Revised Standard Version Bible,
copyright © 1989 by the Division of Christian Education of the National
Council of Churches of Christ in the USA and used by permission.

Contents

Editor's Note · *vii*

Foreword by Walter Brueggemann · *ix*

Introduction · 1

1 Moses the Man · 5

2 The Call of Moses · 15

3 The First and Second Commandments · 28

4 God's Will as Made Manifest in Law · 45

5 From Promise to Fulfillment · 68

Bibliography · 89

Further Reading · 92

Scripture Index · 95

Editor's Note

I offer this new edition of Gerhard von Rad's volume on Moses to a new and wider audience than it originally received. I have a great appreciation for von Rad's contribution to Old Testament studies as well as his ability to take the most sophisticated research and present it in a way that broader audiences can appreciate.

Rather than simply reprinting the 1960 edition of this work, I thought it expedient to prepare a new edition. The original English-language edition included numerous awkward English phrases, it used the older RSV translation of the Bible for quotations, and it included very few footnotes and no bibliography. So what I have done in preparing this edition is:

- used the NRSV for biblical quotations, but read "Yahweh" for NRSV's "the LORD"

- inserted headings throughout the chapters

- added footnotes in order to indicate other works by von Rad that treat these issues in more depth, especially his *Old Testament Theology* and commentaries on Genesis and Deuteronomy

- added a few additional citations where the reader may find more detailed treatments; all my additional notes are marked [Ed.]

- provided a bibliography for the secondary works cited

- provided lists of books for further reading on: Moses, the Ten Commandments and the Law, and Additional Works by Gerhard von Rad

- invited Walter Brueggemann to write a new foreword.

K. C. Hanson
April 2011

Foreword

The decision of Cascade Books (U.S.) and James Clarke (UK) to republish *Moses* by Gerhard von Rad is a most welcome one. Gerhard von Rad is likely the most important Old Testament interpreter of the twentieth century, one whose influence in critical study and in theological exposition continues even now in powerful ways. This little book, first published in 1940 and first translated into English in 1960, is a gem that brings together in quite accessible ways samples von Rad's daring interpretation and his courageous faith.

In this book von Rad appeals to some of his most important critical studies that made him a defining force in the discipline. He makes that appeal to his earlier work without calling attention to it and without making matters especially complex. When we consider that the book was first published in 1940, we are plunged into that dangerous context in which von Rad did some of his most important work. In the wake of the Barmen Declaration of 1934 and in the midst of the Confessing Church in Germany that stood opposed, as best it could, to National Socialism, von Rad had to work out a way to continue to teach and interpret the Old Testament in a political context where hostility to anything Jewish was broad and deep. In 1938 he published his programmatic essay, "The Form-Critical Problem of the Hexateuch," in which he proposed that the theological *Leitmotif* of Genesis–Joshua was the theme of God's promise to Israel that was fulfilled in the gift of the land of promise. That is, he saw a connection in the tradition between the promise of Genesis to the ancestors and the tales of conquest in the book of Joshua. Behind that sweep of promise to fulfillment was von Rad's defining hypothesis about the "credo" in which he identified a succinct statement of the faith of ancient Israel that centered in the events around Moses, most especially the Exodus and the land promise, traditions that were filled out by the covenant of Mt. Sinai.

Many of the critical assumptions with which von Rad worked are no longer sustainable, especially since current scholarship is in a mood to date everything in the Old Testament quite late, whereas von Rad, in an earlier scholarly context, had assumed an earlier dating for the text. But even if his critical assumptions are no longer persuasive, the theological insight he had about the faith claims of the text continue to shape much of the discussion in Old Testament studies concerning the faith of ancient Israel.

Because he was a Lutheran, it is not surprising that von Rad focused on the theme of "law and gospel" a topic that for a Lutheran is unavoidable in the Sinai tradition. Because von Rad wanted to preserve and affirm the cruciality of the Old Testament for Christian faith, he could not treat "the law," that is the commandments of Sinai, as simply a foil for the gospel according to the popular temptation to equate Old Testament–New Testament with "law–grace."

Rather he judged that the God of Israel is the God of "holy freedom" who repeatedly "reveals that his name is a name of inviolable freedom." He is able to affirm, moreover, that the God who speaks the commandments of Sinai is "the God of grace." He said that with reference to God's self-disclosure as "the God of the exodus" as a premise of the first commandment. Thus the commandments are treated by von Rad as for the emancipatory impulse of God over against the economic oppression and coercive "naturalism" of Pharaoh. There is no doubt that his exposition is a fine exegetical offer, and von Rad is to be recognized as a first-rate reader of texts. But the point is even sharper when we recall that his focus is on commandments 1 and 2: "No other gods, no grave images." He offered that exposition of the commandments in the context of German National Socialism that was making an idol of the state and of the "Aryan race." Thus in context von Rad shows the way in which the commandments constitute a ground for resistance to the ideology of National Socialism, a resistance that is also implied in his credo hypothesis of 1938, for he understood the "credo" as a place to stand against the dominant ideology of the state.

Von Rad was, at the same time, attentive to the danger of preempting the Old Testament for Christian faith and thus overriding its clear Jewish formulation and intention. But he did not overstep that boundary by imposing the Christian gospel on the Old Testament, but saw that the God of Israel who saves is indeed the God of good news who enacts emancipatory victories against coercive powers in the history of Israel.

All of which is to say that we should not read this little book "innocently." It sparkles and snaps with strong interpretive impulses that reflect on von Rad's courage and his clear-headedness about the appeal to its radical promises and its equally radical claims. Whatever we can now say about the "historicity of Moses," a matter now greatly vexed in Old Testament studies, von Rad understood well the continuing contemporeneity of the traditions that cluster around Moses, both as promise and as demand (*Gabe* and *Aufgabe*). These are radical invitations to be in the world differently. There is, of course, no obvious one-to-one correlation between the dangers that von Rad faced in Germany in his time and the dangers now faced by twenty-first century readers of his words. Nor is there an obvious one-to-one correlation between the ancient dangers of Israel and our contemporary dangers, and von Rad clearly understood that one cannot easily slide from one to the other. His own work shows the difficult way of interpretation in connecting from one context of danger to another that requires interpretive skill and grace. In his work von Rad makes and implies connections between "then and now" for his own day, even as his book suggests connections between "then and now" in our contemporary day of reading von Rad again. His little book, read knowingly, invites the reader to faith and risk and resolve.

Thus he wrote of the Jubilee Year:

> Man thinks he can treat the land as his own possession; he grasps at all the mysterious powers of the fertile soil, at the treasures of the earth, and he forgets God, who gave all this to him. He regards the land as his own domain, which he can

> exploit in all directions exactly as he pleases. He
> can buy land and sell it; he can let it for a longer
> or shorter period, exactly as circumstances de-
> mand. But over against man's arbitrary assertion
> of his claim to possession of the land, God sets
> up his claim to be the true owner of it.

Von Rad exposited that ancient subversive mandate in the midst of the German reach for *Lebensraum* at the expense of other peoples, precisely because the land could be regarded as a "possession." Now we read von Rad in the midst of military adventurisms and insatiable expansionism accompanied by a deep environmental crisis that seems to have no limit. We continue to regard the land (and its oil!) as a legitimate "possession." The force of such an ideology continues as does—von Rad would surely say—the promise of an alternative. The reappearance of von Rad, through this book, in the midst of our interpretive work is a welcome one—attention must be paid!

Walter Brueggemann
Columbia Theological Seminary
April 4, 2011

Introduction

The Old Testament is a very ancient book. Not only that—
it took a very long time to write. Many of its great stories
were told over and over again and written down at different times. Naturally each age added something of its own,
according to its own understanding of the story. This is as
true of Moses as it is of other great characters of the Old
Testament. Much of what we know of him comes from the
writing, not of those who lived at the same time as Moses,
but of those who lived in later eras. In the narratives, as we
now have them, we see the figure of this great man as it was
reflected in the spirit and the faith of those later eras.

    This means that we have no full biography of Moses;
still less do we have any account of him written in terms of
"strict historical method." But God's self-revelation to the
people of Israel was inseparably connected with his name.
This revelation was felt to have full authority for every later
era, right up to the end of the Old Testament period. And
so it came about that people of all these later eras felt that
they too were concerned in the history of Moses; the ancient traditions that spoke of him were carefully preserved
and passed on from one age to the next.

Now even a reader who does not read very carefully can observe that the figure of Moses and the office that he held are not depicted in exactly the same way in all the stories. There is nothing surprising in this. The portraits that later eras formed of Moses were naturally influenced by the spirit and the outlook of each age, and that means that they differ in detail from one another. One period stresses one aspect of the person and message of Moses, another period a different aspect. One group finds the essential thing in the stern and even terrifying element in the work of Moses; on others we see the impression left by the suffering that lay below the surface of his life and by his service as the mediator between God and his people. But, though these interpretations differ among themselves, each one has without doubt caught something that is true and valid in relation to Moses.

These later writers had in their minds questions and needs and answers to questions related to their own experiences, as they tried to follow Moses in the path of faith. The traditions about him were not stored in archives throughout the centuries; they were passed on as living traditions from mouth to mouth and from soul to soul. Now a picture handed on like this from generation to generation cannot remain unaltered. It is bound to be affected by the experiences of faith that the people of God have passed through in one period or another; in this way it may even come to be a more complete portrait than it was, just because it has been enriched by the discoveries and experiences of later eras. Thus it comes about that what we find in the books of the Old Testament includes something of Israel's own picture of itself and of its history. Consequently, Moses, as he is presented to us, rises to gigantic stature; he surpasses the limits of ordinary human capacity; he stands as a colossus high above all others. And yet, for all that, here is the true and genuine figure of a man, a figure that has power to move us by its very humanity.

But we have not yet come to the most important point of all. Not a single one of all these stories, in which Moses is the central figure, was really written about Moses. Great as was the veneration of the writers for this man to whom God had been pleased to reveal himself, in all these stories it is not Moses himself, Moses the man, but God who is the central figure. God's words and God's deeds, these are the things that the writers intend to set forth. We shall find that this principle applies to all the early narratives of Israel; they are stories of God's great acts of salvation, of his enduring patience, and also of his judgments and vengeance; in no single case is a man—even the very greatest among the sons of men—the central figure. The aim of all these stories is to render honor to God, to glorify God's deeds, God's patience, and the faithfulness that God has been pleased to reveal. In other words, all the stories about Moses bear testimony to God. In them people are not presented in any ideal fashion; on the contrary they are realistically shown in every aspect of their human nature. Thus we should not be surprised to find that human imperfection casts deep shadows even upon these people, who were the recipients of the revelation of the living God; and that truth demands that the failures of these great people should be unsparingly shown up. If we realize this, we are less likely to make the mistake of imagining that the people about whom these stories were written were the really important actors in them.

Since Moses is not the principal actor in the Old Testament stories about him, then, we shall not make him the principal character in our book. First we shall sketch in broad outline the picture of Moses that has been handed down to us in the various strands of the tradition. But once this is done, we shall go on to consider the principal features in that revelation of God associated with his name.

1

Moses the Man

Several times the one with whom we are here concerned is referred to just as "the man Moses" (Exod 32:1, 23; Num 12:3). A strangely simple way of speaking of one who, according to the tradition of later times, combined in his own person almost all imaginable honors of religion and state alike. Was he not at the same time priest and leader and prophet and lawgiver and military commander of his people?[1] Yet, alongside all those titles of honor that a grateful posterity bestowed upon him, this simple description also has its importance and its special significance. Moses was a man, a human being. He was not a saint, an ascetic, one who had stripped himself of all ordinary human feelings. Neither was he a hero in the sense in which that word was ordinarily understood in ancient times. Certainly he was in no way a demi-god. He is indeed presented as a figure of incomparable greatness. But the neat and exact

1. [Ed.] For an extended analysis of the Moses traditions, see von Rad, *Old Testament Theology*, vol. 1, 289–96. See also the works by George W. Coats in the bibliography.

precision with which the dividing line between him and God is always made clear is one of the most admirable features of these narratives. There was nothing divine about Moses. Therefore neither the men of his own time nor the men of later times ever offered to him such worship as is offered to God alone. He was "the man Moses."

Moses's Anger

It sometimes almost looks as though the tradition deliberately goes out of its way to emphasize the human features in the picture of this great man. One trait is especially characteristic of him. From time to time a wild, fierce anger blazes up in him. Under such an impulse he slays the Egyptian who was beating one of his fellow countrymen. This uncontrolled outbreak of passion does not serve as the spark that sets in motion the freeing of Israel from Egypt; it is just the violent action of a man who has not yet heard the call of God. The only result of it is that Moses has to become an exile. But even later, even when he is the man whom God has invested with authority, this furious anger still bursts forth from time to time. When Moses comes down from the mountain and sees the abomination of the worship of the golden calf, in his anger he casts down the tables written with the finger of God and shatters them. He is unwilling to bring to a people so deeply mired in idolatry the revelation of the commandments of God.

On one occasion, the way in which Moses speaks to God does not stop short of downright irreverence. He is at the end of his tether. The giant has broken down under the weight of his commission; he argues with God, he wishes to fling back in his face the task that he has laid upon him:

> Why have you treated your servant so badly . . . that you lay the burden of all this people on me? Did I conceive all this people? Did I give birth to them, that you should say to me, "Carry them in your bosom, as a nurse carries the sucking child," to the land that you promised on oath to their ancestors? . . . I am not able to carry all this people alone, for they are too heavy for me. If this is the way you are going to treat me, put me to death at once . . . and do not let me see my misery. (Num 11:10–15)

And God has mercy on his servant in his despair. Seventy elders are to be brought out to the tent of meeting in order that they may help Moses in his task of governing the people. But for this they need the gift of the Spirit of God; so God takes a part of the Spirit that rests upon Moses and distributes it among these seventy men. Then the unexpected happens: no sooner has the spirit of Moses come upon these men than they fall into a strange state of excitement and ecstasy, which seems as though it is going to have no end (Num 11:24–30). So immense was the power of the Spirit as it rested upon Moses that even a small fragment of it was enough to drive other people completely out of the ordinary balance of their minds. Even the crumbs from Moses's inspiration were a weight too heavy for their mind and spirit to carry. Think then how wonderful Moses must have been! He was able calmly to bear the tremendous weight of the possession of the Spirit, and still to continue to live as a normal human being.

Moses as the Servant of the Lord

In the mirror of this story we can see clearly the reflection of what Moses really was. He was "the man Moses"—nothing more than that. But God had called him, revealed himself to him, and in no ordinary measure had given to him the endowment of the Spirit. Thus he has become "the man of God." "Man of God"—this is his epithet (Deut 33:1; Josh 14:6), or even more clearly "Servant of Yahweh" (Josh 1:1). Servant of Yahweh—the one who no longer belongs to himself. One who bears this label cannot act in independence, cannot speak his own words or walk in his own ways; it is another who has girded him This was the way in which his people thought of him. Of course they knew that Moses was of their own flesh and blood; yet they never boasted of the fact, that their people had produced so great a man as this. He was indeed of their own kindred; but it was God who had given him the gift of his holy Spirit, had enlightened him. It was as a result of this enlightenment, this giving of the Spirit, that Moses had once for all been drawn over to the side of God, caught away from the sphere in which the rest of the people lived.

Should it surprise us that such a man as this could not be popular? With quite horrifying obstinacy, the people countered the work and the service of Moses with murmurings, with hostility, even with open rejection.[2] At one moment, in their faint-heartedness, they completely lose confidence in him and desire to return to Egypt: "Is it because there are no graves in Egypt that you have taken us

2. Exod 5:20–21; 14:11–12; 16:2–3; 17:2–3; Num 11:1–6; 12:1–2; 13:31; 14:1–4; 16:1–3; 20:1–5; 21:5.

away to die in the wilderness?" (Exod 14:11; see Num 14:3). At times, as in the story of Korah, they contest the unique character of the calling and office of Moses; they lay claim to equal rights with him, and to such immediate access to the presence of God as he enjoys (Numbers 16). It is important to notice that, when his right to exercise this office is called in question, Moses does not speak on his own behalf; he leaves his vindication entirely to God (Num 16:5). He is not concerned to maintain his own preeminence; he does not cling to the gift of the Spirit as though it were his own peculiar possession. When the seventy elders fell into that state of enthusiastic excitement, and Joshua urged Moses to forbid such behavior, Moses simply said, "Are you jealous for my sake? Would that all Yahweh's people were prophets, and that Yahweh would put his spirit upon them!" (Num 11:29).

On the day of Pentecost the gift of the Holy Spirit was given to all the faithful [Acts 2]. But in the time of Moses that was still a distant event, and so it was his fate to stand in unimaginable loneliness between God and the people. He was alone in his moments of success; he was alone, too, in those times in which people showed him all too plainly that he wearied them. In this respect Moses was truly a forerunner of the Christ.

So in the story of Sinai, in an unforgettable picture, we see him climbing the mountain, disappearing from human eyes, entering into the clouds, drawing ever nearer to the presence of God:

> Then Moses went up on the mountain, and the cloud covered the mountain. The glory of Yahweh settled on Mount Sinai . . . Now the ap-

> pearance of the glory of Yahweh was like a de-
> vouring fire on the top of the mountain in the
> sight of the people of Israel. Moses entered the
> cloud, and went up on the mountain. Moses was
> on the mountain for forty days and forty nights.
> (Exod 24:15–18)

And when he came down again to join the throng of men below, he had was a changed man, even in his outward appearance. During those long days and nights he had been exposed to the splendor of God—and now something of that brightness remained upon his face. That refraction, that reflection, of the light of God was so piercing that the Israelites could not endure it; they shrank back before him and fled. Only then did Moses realize that his face was bright with a supernatural splendor. He himself had been unaware of it; so deeply had he entered into God's world of light, so completely had he been withdrawn from the sinful world of humans. Only when he had placed a veil before his face could ordinary people draw near to him (Exod 34:29–35).

We may cite one other story as evidence of the loneliness of Moses. The tent of meeting was regularly erected outside the camp. This was the place where God was pleased to reveal himself in speech; thus it was the holy and dangerous place in which the encounter between God and people took place. But this was not an encounter for which any and everyone was qualified. Moses, and Moses alone, was chosen to endure it, and then to pass on the message of God to the people. And so, when Moses prepared himself to enter again on that hard way and went out through the camp to the tent of meeting, everyone came out and stood at the door of his tent. No one could accompany him, but everyone followed him with their eyes. And when he had gone out and reached the tent, and the cloud had descended upon it, all those in the camp fell down upon their faces and worshipped. And there God spoke with Moses—and the narrator records this as something entirely out of the ordinary—"as one speaks to a friend" (Exod 33:7–11).[3]

As the people of the old covenant continued to think deeply of Moses and his career, they became ever more aware of the hidden burden of suffering that was laid upon this man of God. How much, they thought, must such a man have suffered, standing as he did alone between God and the people, and bearing such a weight of responsibility! In the book of Deuteronomy we see Moses as it were standing between the people and the fiery wrath of God. Forty days and forty nights he lay in the presence of God, praying and fasting for the sin of the people. When he learned of the sin that they had committed in the matter of the golden calf, once again he prayed before God for forty days, and ate no bread nor drank water. Here Moses is seen in the clearest light as the great intercessor. Even more even than that—he suffers on behalf of the people and for their sake.[4]

Moses's Death

This aspect of the service of Moses comes out most clearly in the interpretation that is given in Deuteronomy of his death. Naturally, Moses would have wished to go over

3. [Ed.] On the tent of meeting, see von Rad, *Old Testament Theology*, vol. 1, 234–38.

4. Deut 9:7–21, 25–29; see also 1:34–37; 4:21–24.

Jordan with his people, and to enter into the land of promise; he goes so far as to plead with God to grant him this grace:

> O Lord Yahweh, you have only begun to show your servant your greatness and your might . . . Let me cross over to see the good land beyond the Jordan, that good hill country and the Lebanon. (Deut 3:24–25)

But God sternly cuts him short. Here he must die, a death of expiation for the sins of the people: "But Yahweh was angry with me on your account and would not heed me. Yahweh said to me, 'Enough from you! Never speak to me of this matter again'" (Deut 3:26). And so Moses died, as lonely in his death as he had always been in his life (Deuteronomy 34). His death is shrouded in mystery: "his sight was unimpaired, and his vigor had not abated" (Deut 34:7). He, the shepherd and the leader of the people, is not allowed to set foot within the promised land; it is difficult to imagine a harder fate than this.[5]

And yet the story of the death of Moses does not end in lamentation or complaint. For God was with Moses in his death. He is given something far better than hope, for hope always has in it an element of uncertainty. With unveiled eyes and with undimmed spirit Moses sees the fulfillment of the promise. God showed him the whole land of Palestine. Towards the west, his glance swept over the whole land as far as the Great Sea; to the north he beheld the mountains of Galilee; before him lay Jericho, the city of Palm Trees, and to the left were the wide expanses of Judah

5. On the death of Moses, see von Rad, *Deuteronomy*, 209–10; and also Olson, *Deuteronomy and the Death of Moses*.

and the Negev, where the patriarchs had lived in their tents. The narrative tells us nothing of the thoughts and feelings of Moses in the closing moments of his life; everything that is merely personal falls into the background in comparison with the fact that the whole fulfillment of the purposes of God is spread out before the eyes of the one who is about to die.

And then God himself buried his servant. No one else was there, and therefore no one could give any information as to the place in which Moses was buried. Thus his people were spared a grievous temptation. It was impossible for them to pay any kind of divine honors to Moses at his grave. For, according to ancient ideas of the veneration to be paid to heroes, the two necessary conditions were the solemn consecration of the grave and the mysterious and continued presence of the spirit of the departed at it.

Let us look back once again on the picture that the people of Israel drew of Moses. This picture tends to throw ever more clearly into relief the features of the mediator, of the servant of God who suffers and dies for his people; and this is a very remarkable characteristic of it.[6] The people of the old covenant, in setting forth this picture of Moses who suffered and offered expiation for the sins of his people, were thereby giving expression to a secret and inward hope. When we read these passages of Deuteronomy, is it not as though we hear the people of Israel say, "It was

6. [Ed.] "Even the death of Moses outside the land of promise—an odd fact which later ages had to explain theologically—was vicarious for Israel. It is because of Israel that Yahweh's great wrath was directed upon Moses, with the result that Yahweh refused to allow him to set foot in the land of promise" (von Rad, *Old Testament Theology*, vol. 1, 295).

fitting" (even more strongly, "it was necessary") "that we should have such a high priest" (Heb 7:26), and that thus the story of Moses becomes a prophecy of that which could be fulfilled only in the coming of Jesus Christ?

2

The Call of Moses

There was nothing exceptional about Moses in the days before God called him. He had had a wonderful education in Egypt; but the writers of the Bible do not depict him as having been particularly pious; he had become a shepherd, just like any number of other shepherds; the only thing that distinguished him from them was that he had had to flee into the land of Midian, and so had become separated from his own people. Of course it is true that that ill-advised act of violence which laid the Egyptian low (Exod 2:11–12) was in strange fashion fitted into the providential purpose of God, since it was there in his refuge in the land of Midian that the call of God was to come to him.

Revealing the Divine Name

One day, without any idea of what was to happen to him, Moses had led his flock to Mount Horeb, to the very spot that God had appointed as the place in which his great revelation would be made. There God revealed himself to him in the flame of the burning bush (Exod 3:1–3). Many interpreters have thought that some mysterious truth is hinted at in the fact that God revealed himself in a burning bush; but there is no need to think that this is so.[1] It is unlikely that the narrator had any idea of a hidden and mysterious truth concealed in the event he records. That was the way in which the story had come down from the earliest times. This was the way in which it had pleased God to make himself manifest in visible form. Far more important from the point of view of our narrator is the very remarkable conversation that now ensues:

> Then Yahweh said, "I have observed the misery of my people who are in Egypt; I have heard their cry . . . and I have come down to deliver them from the Egyptians, and to bring them up out of that land to a good and broad land, a land flowing with milk and honey . . . So come, I will send you to Pharaoh to bring my people, the Israelites, out of Egypt." But Moses said to God, "Who am I that I should go to Pharaoh, and bring the Israelites out of Egypt?" He said, "I will be with you." . . . But Moses said to God, "If I come to the Israelites and say to them, 'The God of your ancestors has sent me to you,' and they ask me, 'What is his name?' what shall I say to them?" God said to Moses, "I AM WHO I AM." (Exod 3:7–14)

1. Older interpreters took the flame, which enveloped the bush but did not consume it, to be a symbol of the divine holiness, which descends upon humans but does not destroy them. It may be that we do not need to look further than the fact that the Hebrew word for bush (*seneh*) points in concealed fashion to Sinai, the name of the mountain at which the great revelation of God is to be given.

What did Moses mean by the question that he asked of God in the name of the people? What is in their minds, when they ask to know the name of God? One thing is clear—they are not interested in the name simply as a word. If they say that they want to know the name, this means in fact that they want to know something of the nature and of the being of God. A God who has no name is, in point of fact, no better than an unknown God. People in antiquity took it for granted that we are surrounded on all sides by super-human powers, the nature of which is beyond our capacity fully to grasp. But who are these powers? That is the urgent question. Is one to think of them as unfriendly deities that begrudge him peace and prosperity? Or can one think of them as being favorable?

To find an answer to this question was at all times a matter of the highest interest. It is for this reason that Moses at once asks to be allowed to know the name of the God who is revealing himself to him. People cannot pay personal reverence and worship to an unknown God. They can really worship only a God whom they know, who has revealed himself; and therefore he requires the knowledge of his name.

But another and a different idea underlies this question about the name. People long for the revelation of God, not only for God's sake, in order that God may be worshipped and adored, but in reality far more for their own sake than for God's. It is because they need God that they desire to call upon him. Just because they have such an intense need of God, they want to get God permanently into their own power. They want to have a God who in a sense becomes part of themselves; they want to put God to work for them. In certain circumstances, so it was believed, they could get the deity so completely under their own control that they could make arbitrary use of it—then we say that they are practicing magic. In a word, the question of Moses about the name of God is the expression at the same time of the human need for God and of human impudence in relation to God.

And now—we wait in breathless suspense—what is God going to answer to this most urgent of all man's questions in the field of religion? "I will be that which I will be." The form of expression in Hebrew makes it plain that this mysterious phrase is intended to paraphrase and to explain the hidden name of God, YHWH.[2] But is this really an explanation? Is it not an evasion rather than an answer? Yes, this is the first impression that is surely to be left upon our minds—God is withdrawing himself from the importunity of humans. He does not allow anyone to lay claim to him, as humans would so gladly do; he preserves his own freedom and the mystery of his being. But we have gone only halfway towards expounding this utterance, if we see in it no more than God's refusal to answer people's questions. The Hebrew word we translated above "I will be" signifies rather "to be present," or even "to take place." Its reference, therefore, is rather to being in action, in activity, than to being at rest; and therefore we can say with certainty that the reference here is not to God "as he is in himself," but to God "as he turns himself towards humans." This is, then, a word spoken by a God who condescends to humans, who makes them aware of his willingness to help them. We might

2. In later eras, Jews did not pronounce this sacred name, and this is the reason it is often written with the consonants only and without the vowels.

almost go so far as to translate it, "I will be for you that which I will be for you"; some have thought that it could better be rendered, "I will manifest myself to be that which I will manifest myself to be."[3]

If God sends to people living in misery the message that he will show himself active according to his own free decision, from the first moment the affirmation is a word of comfort, an assurance that God is "the One who is always there"; perhaps it is not too much to say that it is an assurance of the faithfulness of God. There are two points, then, to be noted: God condescends to humans, he reveals himself to humans as the God who is there to help—the constant, active God. But at the same time he reveals that he is completely free in his own actions. He will always be Yahweh; he never gives himself up into the hands of humans, and he will never put himself at the service of their purposes.

Manoah and the Angel of the LORD

Two stories in the Old Testament set out simply and clearly this truth that perhaps is a little difficult for us to grasp. The first is in Judges 13. God had appeared to the wife of Manoah in the form of "the angel of Yahweh," and had foretold the birth of a son, who was later to be called Samson. Clearly Manoah has no idea that it was God himself who had appeared to his wife—he is simply convinced that some heavenly being or other has visited her; his only regret is that his wife had not shown herself a little cleverer, and so

3. [Ed.] On the divine name, see von Rad, *Old Testament Theology*, vol. 1, 10–11, 179–87; see also Freedman et al., "יהוה YHWH."

had failed to bring this divine being into such a relationship with herself as would make it possible to make use of him. So Manoah prays that the manifestation may be repeated. In answer to his prayer, the angel appears again to the woman alone. This time, however, Manoah, who has hurried up in breathless haste, succeeds in meeting the angel, and the following conversation takes place:

> "Are you the man who spoke to this woman?"
> And he said, "I am." . . . Manoah said to the angel
> of Yahweh, "Allow us to detain you, and prepare
> a kid for you." (Judg 13:11, 15)

"Allow us detain you." With touching simplicity Manoah gives expression to that eager desire that lies hidden in the heart of everyone—to have God for one's own, to hold him as tight as possible. The angel is unwilling to accede to Manoah's importunity. But Manoah is far from giving up the struggle:

> Manoah said to the angel of Yahweh, "What is
> your name, so that we may honor you when your
> words come true?" (v. 17)

Here once again we trace the hidden self-seeking, which decks itself out with a mask of piety. But God turns the question back on Manoah:

> And the angel of Yahweh said to him, "Why do
> you ask my name? It is too wonderful." (v. 18)

Even then, Manoah is not prepared to give up his purpose; he hastens to provide a sacrifice. But the angel vanishes in the flame of the altar and leaves Manoah half-dead with terror.

This brief narrative is extremely important. The narrator knows something of the tremendous strength of that human impulse that makes people, even genuinely religious people, want to get God under their own control. But he well knows also that this is idolatry. This is not the way that a person can draw near to the living God; if he tries to do so, he is doing violence to God's sacred freedom. Once again God reveals that his name is a name of inviolable freedom.

Jacob at the Jabbok River

The second story, found in Genesis 32:22–32, tells us something rather different.[4] Jacob is on his way home from exile to the land of his ancestors. He is weighed down by the weight of shame that he feels in relation to his brother Esau. Night has fallen. He has sent his family and his possessions over the Jabbok River, "and a man wrestled with him until the breaking of the day." The story leaves us in no doubt that it is with the Lord God himself that Jacob is dealing, as he wrestles with this nightly visitor. And yet, grievous as was this conflict by night, and filled with terror as Jacob must have been, we find that the desire that springs up in his heart is exactly the same as that which was in the heart of Manoah. Half-dead as he is with strain and anxiety, Jacob can still say to God, "Tell me, I pray, your name."

This story makes plain to us that, whatever the depth of need into which one may fall, nothing can reduce a person to such humility that one is healed of this kind of

4. [Ed.] For a fuller treatment of this passage, see von Rad, *Genesis*, 319–26; see also Westermann, *Genesis 12–36*, 512–21; and Brueggemann, *Genesis*, 260–74.

impudent desire to take hold of God for his own purposes. Once again God turns Jacob's question back upon him:

> But he said, "Why is it that you ask my name?"
> And there he blessed him. So Jacob called the
> name of the place Peniel, saying, "For I have seen
> God face to face, and yet my life is preserved."
> (Gen 32:29–30)

What a pair of stories! In each case, the human's question is treated as unseemly, and no answer is given to it; and yet, "There he blessed him." On the one side God manifests the freedom that rejects every effort on the part of humans to take possession of him; and on the other he manifests his faithfulness: he is the same God who said to Moses, "I will be for you that which I will be for you."

For His Name's Sake

We must not lose sight of the fact that the people of the old covenant did in fact learn a name for God, the holy name Yahweh, and that they accepted this name as being in itself the guarantee of that revelation of deliverance that God had been pleased to give them. So this name was very far from being just a name that a man can learn and then there is no more to it. No, this name stood for and summed up the gift of the whole gracious will of God for his people. In consequence, the constant calling on the name of God—as for instance in the Psalms—is anything but a meaningless liturgical flower of speech:

> he restores my soul.
> He leads me in paths of righteousness
> *for his name's sake.* (Ps 23:3)

This verse, if we expound it rightly, means something like this: "Of myself and from myself I could not venture on such reckless confidence. But God has revealed to his people, in his name, his saving will. That means that on behalf of people he has come forth from his hiddenness, from his unapproachable distance. And the name that we know and on which we can call is the guarantee and assurance that this is so."

Thus we see that, in the faith of the Old Testament, the *name* of God and *his saving will* are inseparably held together. One of the most beautiful of the stories about Moses makes this plain to us yet once more (Exod 33:18–23). God is telling Moses that the time has come when the people must set forth from Sinai and make their way deep into the desert. Is Moses perhaps afflicted by anxiety about the dark way that lies before him? Suddenly from his very heart he utters a request of the most astonishing boldness: "Show me your glory." God must refuse the request of his servant; Moses cannot see the face of God, for no man can see the face of God and live. Yet God is pleased to do something else for him:

> And he said, "I will make all my goodness pass before you, and will proclaim before you my name 'Yahweh'; and I will be gracious to whom I will be gracious, and will show mercy on whom I will show mercy.'" (Exod 33:19)

And then, after the Lord has thus passed by and has held his hand over Moses for his protection, Moses is allowed to see God from behind. When God comes down to a person, that person cannot watch him, cannot look upon him directly as he is at work; but to look on the wondrous works of God, after they have taken place—that is within human capacity. We can readily think of a parallel; when God set to work on the creation of the first woman, he caused a deep sleep to fall upon the man (Gen 2:21). In the same way, when God came down to make His covenant with Abraham, he first caused Abraham to sink into deep sleep, into a deep and terrifying darkness (Gen 15:12).

Israel was well aware of the distance that separates man from God. It knew that, if a person was allowed to look on the depths of the mysteries of God, he would simply be destroyed. It is for this reason that Moses cannot behold the glory of God. But, for all that, God does not withdraw himself from his servant. What he does grant to him is the revelation of his name. Now the name of God, as we have seen, means the side of God that is turned toward humanity, the saving aspect of God; or, as this passage quite clearly puts it, it means that God is gracious to the one to whom he is gracious. What else is this but another way of saying "I will be to you what I will be to you"—the word of the freedom and of the faithfulness of God? We may remember the answer that came to the apostle Paul in rather similar circumstances: "My grace is sufficient for you" (2 Cor 12:9).

The Sanctity of Yahweh's Name

We have studied a number of passages in the Old Testament in our attempt to understand all that is implied in this phrase "the name of God." Now perhaps we are in a position to understand the immense importance of the command, "You shall not make wrongful use of the name of Yahweh your God" (Exod 20:7a). The purpose of this command is to say "no," thoroughly and completely, to that desire that lies so deep in the heart of man, the desire to infringe the freedom of God; and that means here the freedom of the God who graciously condescends to humans.[5]

The particular way in which people try to get God into their power is not the important thing. In those early days people were sorely tempted to call in the magician, in order to assure themselves with his help that they had gotten the invisible under their control. The same thing has happened from time to time even in the history of the Christian Church. This is perhaps the coarsest of the ways in which one can try to misuse God and the revelation of his grace. But, from the time of Moses on, among the people of the old covenant, to act or think in this way was regarded as a very grave infringement of the freedom of God: "Am I a God near by, says Yahweh, and not a God far off?" (Jer 23:23).

So the name of God in the Old Testament brings us face to face with a strange and perplexing mystery. People know that name and utter it; and yet, in relation to it, they are like someone standing on the edge of a precipice. Here is a name. Implied in this name is a revelation of God filled to the brim with grace and with God's freedom to forgive; and yet at the same time this revelation entices a person, in

---

5. [Ed.] "Originally the term שׁוא ['wrongful use' or 'in vain'] may well have signified magic, and it is conceivable that even in Israel people were at times liable to use Yahweh's name for sinister purposes dangerous to the community. But this commandment was probably in the main directed against false swearing, for every genuine oath was accompanied by invocation of the deity (Lev. 19:12). Further, to hallow the name of Yahweh was tantamount in itself to acknowledging the uniqueness and exclusiveness of the cult of Israel *per se*." Von Rad, *Old Testament Theology*, vol. 1, 183–84.

the secret depths of one's being, to try to lay violent hands upon it; it seems to stimulate that rebellious element that is present in every person. Is it surprising that in the end the problem was solved by taking this name out of the mouths of people and absolutely forbidding them ever to utter it?

But this was not in reality a solution. It only meant that the mystery was sealed up. Then came the time when the books of the Old Testament were collected and bound together by the iron clasp of the canon; and so the inheritance and the harvest of the whole story of God's salvation, as it had been wrought in the days of the Old Testament, was shut away and sealed up in a book. And at its heart, like the soul and the secret of the meaning of the book, lay the mystery of the most holy name of God. Who will break the seal and reveal the mystery?

Revealing the Mystery

So we turn our attention to that moment when, in the synagogue at Nazareth (Luke 4:16–21), the scroll of the ancient Scriptures was handed to Jesus. When he had read the chosen passage, everyone's eyes were fastened on him. "Then he began to say to them, 'Today this scripture has been fulfilled in your hearing'" (4:21). And so he taught the disciples to find all the places in the Scriptures that had been written concerning him: "Then beginning with Moses and all the prophets, he interpreted to them the things about himself in all the scriptures" (Luke 24:27). "You search the scriptures because you think that in them you have eternal life; and it is they that testify on my behalf" (John 5:39). Really, only he had the authority to open the Old Testament and to break the seals that had been placed upon it. Is it not in him that the salvation of God, and also God's power to rule all things according to his will, have been revealed? Is it not true that in Jesus Christ God has revealed himself as far exceeding everything that people have thought about him, and everything that men have desired of him?

Moreover, do we not see in the life of Jesus Christ exactly that which we have seen in the Old Testament to be true in relation to the name of God—that humans are tempted to take possession of him for themselves? In him too they have tried to infringe the freedom of God's action—in the first place in that they tried to take possession of him and to make him a king (John 6:15); and in the second place in that they nailed him to the cross. So one who believes in Jesus cannot but see the deep connection, when we read the Bible as the record of God's saving activity, between Jesus Christ and the name of God in the Old Testament. As we look back from the New Testament to the Old, we may be inclined to feel that the holy name of God in the Old Testament is as it were temporarily taking the place of the Lord who is yet to come.

3

The First and Second Commandments

Research has made it reasonably certain that, after the settlement of the twelve tribes in Canaan, the Ten Commandments had a place of special honor in the great autumn festival, which was known as the Feast of Tabernacles. In this festival the people of Israel entered each year upon a renewal of their relationship with God. As the high peak of the festival the Ten Commandments were ceremonially recited by the priest. And in this solemn act God asserted anew his claim upon the people; the Ten Commandments are the proclamation of his total sovereignty over them.

The First Commandment

We must study the first commandment at considerable length, because it is the head and chief of all the commandments.[1] We might even say that the almost countless laws

1. [Ed.] For further discussion of the first commandment, see von Rad, *Old Testament Theology*, vol. 1, 202–12; also Capetz, "The First Commandment as a Theological and Ethical Principle."

and rules that follow do no more than expand and unfold this one commandment in one direction or another:

> I am Yahweh your God, who brought you out
> of the land of Egypt, out of the house of slavery.
> You shall have no other gods before me. (Exod
> 20:2–3)

If we are rightly to understand the meaning of the commandment, we must take seriously the addition, "who brought you out of the land of Egypt." The God who speaks here is the God of grace. From the point of view of ordinary history, the deliverance of Israel out of Egypt is an event of extraordinarily small importance. These half-nomadic tribes had gone down to Egypt, and had there been compelled to accept the status of serfs. Now they have managed to acquire their freedom. But the pious folk of the Old Testament, up till the very latest time, regarded this outwardly unimportant event as the moment at which the people was brought into being as a people; here God's saving will has been revealed; here for the first time God has glorified himself, that is, has made plain before the eyes of all his gracious sovereignty in human history.

That additional clause in the first commandment tells us that the God who speaks in this way is not just some god or other, he is the very God who has come down to free his own people. He has called them out of the house of bondage in order to lead them into that freedom that consists in obedience to himself.

God has given his people freedom. But this freedom means before all else that Israel must separate itself from the worship of every other god. It has rightly been pointed out by scholars that Moses is here thinking not so much of the gods of the great Eastern religions—Marduk, Ishtar, Re, Osiris, and the rest. The first commandment is concerned in the first place with those powers close at hand—spirits of the dead or demons—to the power of which the people in antiquity attributed so many of the operations and events that influenced their daily lives. If we have recognized this, we shall understand in a new way how important this commandment is for us today. For the real dangers and temptations do not usually come to people from the gods of other religions. They come much more from those nameless powers and forces that people are inclined to accept as exercising some control over the course of history, apart from the will of God, and to which they are therefore inclined to pay divine honors. Martin Luther saw remarkably clearly that what the first commandment asks is the question of confidence—in whom do you really trust? "A god is that to which we look for all good and where we resort for help in every time of need . . . Now I say, whatever your heart clings to and confides in, that is really your God."[2] This confidence in God is broken when one has secret relations with other powers, and perhaps in one's heart ascribes to them more effectiveness and more power to help than one does to the living God.

The faith of the Old Testament carried on this warfare with special bitterness in one direction—against belief in the spirits of the underworld, against demons and spirits of the dead, against soothsaying and necromancy, against every occult practice of this kind. Humans are always exposed to the temptation to think of the spirits of the departed as having now in some way become divine beings,

2. [Ed.] Luther, *Large Catechism*.

and then quite naturally to offer sacrifice to them, "the offerings of the dead," in order to bind them fast to himself and to assure himself of their favor. This temptation was as real to Israel as to any other people. But the religion of the Old Testament at all times condemned such practices as sinful. It had drawn the dividing line sharply and clearly between God and every created thing. It maintained this line as sharply and clearly after death as before it, and would not permit the distinction between God and humanity to be in any way obscured. For this reason it declared the dead and the grave to be unclean, i.e., incapable of being the place or the object of any kind of worship or sacrifice.[3]

The prohibitions set out in Deuteronomy 18 are quite comprehensive:[4]

> When you come into the land that Yahweh your God is giving you, you must not learn to imitate the abhorrent practices of those nations. No one shall be found among you who makes a son or daughter pass through fire, or who practices divination, or is a soothsayer, or an augur, or a sorcerer, or one who casts spells, or consults with ghosts or spirits, or who seeks oracles from the dead. For whoever does these things is abhorrent to Yahweh. (Deut 18:9–12)

The confidence with which the clear line of division is here drawn is really amazing. As with a wave of the hand, magic, necromancy, soothsaying—in a word the whole wide and alluring world of the occult—is swept lock, stock, and barrel out of the field of religion. The Old Testament does

3. Num 19:14–16; see also 5:2; 9:10; Lev 21:1.

4. [Ed.] See von Rad, *Deuteronomy*, 122–25.

not, indeed, deny or question the existence of that darker side of the earthly realm. But it does reject quite firmly the idea that through the mediation of these powers one can enter into any kind of relationship with God, or read the riddle of his will. These powers, whatever they may be, belong to the order of the created and not of the Creator; it is not through their mediation that God draws near to humans. God has been pleased to reveal himself to humans in another and more direct way—in the clear words of the prophet whom he has enlightened. It is there, and there alone, that we are to seek him. And so we recognize once again that wonderful condescension of God to humanity, when the Lord speaks through the mouth of Moses as follows:

> Yahweh your God will raise up for you a prophet like me from among your people; you shall heed such a prophet. (Deut 18:15)

Earlier interpreters took these words as referring to the coming of one particular prophet. But the words can also be taken in the sense that Israel will never be left without a prophet, that the dialogue in which God has engaged with his people is one that will never cease nor fail. In Moses's great speech of farewell there is one phrase that in this connection demands our attention:

> The secret things belong to Yahweh our God, but the revealed things belong to us and to our children forever to observe all the words of this law. (Deut 29:29)

This phrase speaks, once again, of the hidden and unknown forces by which our life is surrounded; and once again it turns human eyes away from that dark side of the world, under the spell of which they are liable again and again to fall. But these words go far beyond what is expressed in the commandment to which we earlier referred. There are regions of the world that humans cannot penetrate; there are mysteries that we cannot solve. But here faith, with incomparable confidence in God, leaves that whole realm of being in his hands. "The secret things belong to Yahweh our God." The first thing that we are to learn from this phrase is certainly that man has no business to look inquisitively into these things and to attempt to master them. But the word goes further; this that is unseen and unknown is not meaningless or subject to arbitrary caprice; it too belongs to God and not to the devil.

How could we live even one single day without the consolation of this knowledge, if we think seriously of the sorrows and perplexities that pile themselves up round about us on every side? The secret things—these are not ours. But the revealed word of God and his commandments—these belong to us. They have been spoken to us by God himself—to our ears and to our hearts—in order that these may become, in the fullest sense of the term, our own most personal possession.

In another passage of this farewell speech Moses is concerned to present the revelation of God to people as something that is really relevant to them, something that is not intended ever to be the source of problems and difficulties:[5]

> Surely, this commandment that I am commanding you today is not too hard for you, nor is it too far away. It is not in heaven, that you should

5. [Ed.] Ibid., 184–85.

> say, "Who will go up to heaven for us, and get
> it for us so that we may hear it and observe it?"
> Neither is it beyond the sea, that you should say,
> "Who will cross to the other side of the sea for
> us, and get it for us so that we may hear it and
> observe it?" No, the word is very near to you; it
> is in your mouth and in your heart for you to
> observe. (Deut 30:11–14)

It would be a very grave error if we were to imagine
that the word spoken to us by God is something distant or
hidden from us. Any kind of ideal after which man strives,
without being able to attain it, must be regarded as a command that summons him from afar. God's salvation and
God's commands, on the contrary, are not something that a
person has to bring within one's reach by one's own efforts.
We are not to imagine that one is to seek out the law of
God; on the contrary, the law of God has come to seek out
humans, in the very place in which he is to be found. Man is
always inclined to think that the word of God is too high for
him, and that he must strain and make tremendous efforts
in order to hear it—and yet all the time it is in reality very
near to his mouth and to his heart.

It is time, however, to return to the first commandment, and the exclusive claim that it makes on behalf of one
God and one only. What we call "exclusiveness" is a modern way of expressing what the Old Testament commonly
calls "the zeal" or "the jealousy" of God. This is a feature of
the Old Testament revelation that many people today reject
with indignation. We are not in a position to parry their
objection by suggesting that this phrase about the jealousy of God occurs only occasionally in the Old Testament,
and that it is therefore not to be regarded as an essential

characteristic of the Old Testament belief in God. The exact contrary is the truth. In all periods, in all the traditions of the Old Testament on every level, this element in its faith plays a great, even a determining, part. For the Old Testament revelation points us to a God who is in no way a neutral power, something like a world-principle or a power of nature. On the contrary; God is here realized as in every respect person and will; in a word, he is an "I" who speaks to humans as to a "thou."

We spoke above of the "zeal" or the "jealousy" of God; and in fact in Hebrew hardly any distinction is made between these two terms. This may help us to understand what is really meant by the words. God is jealous—the prophet Hosea puts it boldly in the words that he is jealous, like a lover, like a bridegroom—that for humans he should be the only God; he is jealous that he and he alone should possess the human heart. God is, therefore, not inclined to share with any other power in the world God's claim to people's love and honor and worship. In Deuteronomy 18:13 we find a command that puts the claim to exclusiveness in its most uncompromising form. The NRSV reads, "You must remain completely loyal to Yahweh your God"; but the Hebrew, literally translated, means, "You shall be entirely (i.e. undividedly) with Yahweh your God."

When later on Israel came to write its own history, the only question asked about each of the kings is this: Was he entirely and undividedly in the service of God (1 Kgs 8:61; 11:4; 15:3, 14)? For it was the judgment of these historians that, in all the ebb and flow of history, Israel had first and last to do with God alone. The destruction of Israel—so we sum up their findings as they looked back on the whole course of history was not due in the last resort to any political power but to God himself. Again and again Israel had tried to evade this decision to be the people of God and nothing else, had tried to turn aside to some easier way.

But again and again, in the course of its history, people of God and prophets had stood before Israel in the way, and had challenged them to take their stand firmly on the side of God. As far back as the time of Joshua, we find Joshua presenting this challenge at the great assembly of the people at Shechem:

> Now therefore revere Yahweh, and serve him in sincerity and in faithfulness; put away the gods that your ancestors served beyond the River and in Egypt, and serve Yahweh. Now if you are unwilling to serve Yahweh, choose this day whom you will serve . . . but as for me and my house, we will serve Yahweh. (Josh 24:14–15)

Centuries later we find the prophet Elijah in a similar situation on Mount Carmel. We are not to imagine that the people had entirely deserted their own God. They still believed themselves to be loyal to him, they still prayed to him; but their heart was not "entirely" with him, it was "divided," since they wished also to maintain friendly relationships with the nature-god Baal. This they regarded as a quite satisfactory situation—a little belief in the God of heaven and at the same time a little belief in nature. But now Elijah the prophet sets himself like a rock in opposition to the people:

> How long will you go limping with two different opinions? If Yahweh is God, follow him; but if Baal, then follow him. (1 Kgs 18:21)

But the God "in whom people trust and on whom they wholly rely" cannot be simply a power whose sphere is that world which lies beyond the reach of our senses, the spiritual world. The great prophets of Israel, with the most penetrating clearness, recognized the true nature of all those earthly forces that people had turned into idols. They carried on a steady campaign against the policy of alliances, against armaments and cavalry; for all these were forms of insurance that Israel felt that it could use in order to evade its obligation of trusting in God and in God's help alone. For Isaiah, faith means to sit still and wait for the God who has risen up to help, and not to frustrate his action by confidence in what one can do for one's self.[6] If only the people will place itself in the hands of God with complete confidence, wonderful things will happen. So on one occasion Isaiah rebukes the people of Jerusalem who, on the threat of an Assyrian invasion, had busied themselves with the fortifications of their city:

> On that day you looked to the weapons of the House of the Forest, and you saw that there were many breaches in the city of David, and you collected the waters of the lower pool. You counted the houses of Jerusalem, and you broke down the houses to fortify the wall . . . But you did not look to him who did it, or have regard for him who planned it long ago. (Isa 22:8–11)

It would be impossible to put the question of trust in God more sharply than the prophet put it in making these demands of his people.

6. Isa 7:4; 30:15.

37

The Second Commandment

In the Old Testament the second commandment runs:

> You shall not make yourself an idol, whether in
> the form of anything that is in heaven above, or
> that is on the earth beneath, or that is in the wa-
> ter under the earth. (Exod 20:4)

In earlier times it was held that this commandment
was given to tell us something about the nature of God himself—that God is spiritual, and that therefore God cannot
dwell in those idols that are made of material things. But in
reality such an interpretation entirely misses the purpose
for which the command was given.[7] Its aim is not to make
a speculative, philosophical declaration concerning the nature of God. It is concerned not with the being of God, but
with the manner in which God reveals himself. Many even
among the heathen had rejected the idea that God can dwell
in an idol, or can even in some way be regarded as identi-
cal with it. But everyone is inclined to exercise an arbitrary
choice as to what they are and what they are not prepared to
accept as divine revelation. Now this, in the sense in which
the Old Testament uses the word, is to make for ourselves
an image of God, since by doing so a person—we repeat,
without really understanding what one is doing—has made
one's self the master and God the servant.

7. [Ed.] For further discussion of the second commandment, see
von Rad, *Old Testament Theology*, vol. 1, 212–19; also Barton, "The
Work of Human Hands."

Creator and Creation

In every era people are equally exposed to the temptation in some way to draw God into the world that they have made, and so to set up some created thing as their god, as the object of their worship. In one case, a person sets up an idol made of some material substance, and under this image pays divine honor to one or other of the mysteries of the world in which one lives. Another person, intellectually better qualified, rejects the idea of representing the object of his worship by a sacred image that his eyes can see. But in reality the difference between the two may not be very great. Of course it is true that the whole creation bears witness to and glorifies God—

> The heavens are telling the glory of God;
>> and the firmament proclaims his handiwork. (Ps 19:1)

But humanity is no longer able to hear this witness in the right way; we tend spontaneously to identify God with the works of his hands; and so we are led astray into a material view of God, to the adoration of some created thing.

This is the great sin, which it is the purpose of the second commandment to exclude, and that in the most radical fashion that can be imagined. Moses belongs to his own time, and he still thinks, as the people of that time thought, of a universe constructed in three stories—heaven, earth, and the waters of chaos under the earth. These three levels of the universe—the whole world of created things, are reviewed together, and it is declared that in them there is nothing, no creature and no form, that can represent God in a manner worthy of him. In all these three levels of the world there is nothing whatever, whether it be original element or fully fashioned creature, that may be mistaken for an immediate manifestation of God and so set up as the object of human worship.

The Golden Calf

This principle is shown forth in the clearest fashion in the story of the golden calf (Exodus 32).[8] Moses is up on the mountain tarrying in the presence of God. The people become impatient. So they turn to the man best qualified to deal with the situation, Aaron the priest, and besiege him with their requests:

> Come, make gods for us, who shall go before us;
> as for this Moses, the man who brought us up
> out of the land of Egypt, we do not know what
> has become of him. (Exod 32:1)

How very revealing this is! This is what the people are, when left to themselves even for a moment. Released only for a short time from the stern discipline of the word of God, they impatiently demand to be provided with an image of God. The desire to be able to worship God in some visible earthly form is one of the deepest instincts of human nature. We cannot bear to live in a world in which there is nothing for us to worship, in which there is not a single idol. We see further that one is quite willing to pay for this worship, that one is prepared to make real sacrifices to make it possible (32:3). And quite naturally people turn to the

8. [Ed.] For an in-depth treatment of Exodus 32, see Childs, *The Book of Exodus*, 553–81.

priest. What else is he there for but to satisfy this universal human desire?

Does this mean, we may then ask, that the people of Israel have entirely fallen away from their own God? Can they claim that, after their sin as before it, they are worshipping the God "who brought us out of the land of Egypt" (32:4)? This is the point at which what is perhaps the most important thing in the whole story is made clear to us. Without doubt, Aaron and the whole people would passionately have denied that they had forsaken their own God. It was their firm intention to worship the same God as they had always worshipped, the God who had revealed himself to them in his great saving acts. They certainly did not imagine that this God dwelt as it were physically in the golden calf that their hands had prepared. What then was the nature of their sin?

The calf, or perhaps rather the bull, was of great importance in the religions of the ancient Near East. In it people worshipped what we would nowadays call the mystery of life, that inexhaustible power of fertility that keeps life going in both men and animals, and carries it forward victoriously beyond the death of the individual. But fertility is not itself the creator; it is no more than a part of the creation.

There are many people today who would not wish to understand the word "God" in "such a narrow sense." Does God not reveal himself in all the wonder and the mystery that surround us? But the Bible tells us that, unless one hearkens to the word of the living God, one falls away helplessly to the worship of something created; that means that one worships God under the figure of some earthly power, which is not God, but belongs to the created world, of which God is thus no longer accepted as the Lord. We have said that these powers and mysteries, which man regards as the revelation of God, belong in fact to the fallen world. The story of the golden calf gives us a clear and unmistakable sign that this is so in the wantonness and unchastity that suddenly take possession of the people (Exod 32:6, 17–20, 25). A strange uproar and wild crying break in on the stillness of the mountain and reach the ears of Moses. It could not be otherwise; there is something dangerously uncontrolled and insubordinate in this kind of worship; for the powers to which man has here surrendered himself are the crude "demonic" powers of the underworld.

In ministering to the people in their falling away into idolatry, the priest has brought an especially heavy burden of guilt upon himself. So Moses asks Aaron:

> What did this people do to you that you have brought so great a sin upon them? (v. 21)

Aaron, the religious professional, should he not have been the first to oppose the people in their wrong desire? His defense of himself is naive—it sounds almost like a schoolboy speaking:

> Do not let the anger of my lord burn hot; you know the people, that they are bent on evil. They said to me, "Make us gods, who shall go before us" . . . So I said to them, "Whoever has gold, take it off"; so they gave it to me, and I threw it into the fire, and out came this calf! (vv. 23–24)

And yet this answer of Aaron is not wholly false. Looking back on it, he himself cannot understand how it all happened that way; everything took place so quickly and unexpectedly—and there they all were absorbed in the worship of an idol!

But it is not always the people of God as a whole who are attacked by the temptation to worship God under the form of some earthly object. Public worship may be completely opposed to any such idea; and yet each individual may be all the time exposed to the attacks of that temptation. He may be taking part quite sincerely in the public worship of the congregation; and yet, for his own personal religious needs, he may have set up a private altar with his own private idol:

> Cursed be anyone who makes an idol or casts an image, anything abhorrent to Yahweh, the work of an artisan, and sets it up in secret. (Deut 27:15)

No doubt this was something that happened fairly often. A man was regularly taking part in the great public acts of worship of the congregation, but at the same time secretly in his own house was carrying on worship before some idol. This meant that, though he recognized his duty to the God whom all worshipped together in the open, he felt himself at the same time under obligation to some power of darkness, to which he believed himself to be indebted for some extra and private blessing. We must not suppose that this commandment has no meaning for Christians today and is therefore superfluous. Probably we are not tempted today to set up graven images or molten images in our own houses and to fall down before them in secret.

Today it is in our hearts that we set up our private altars. The kind of altar that we set up in our hearts may vary very much according to our race and background and class.

But probably there are few Christians, even today, who do not stand in need of this warning.

Let us now take a final look backwards at these two commandments and at what they teach. Only among a people who for a thousand years had been disciplined by these two commandments was it possible that the incarnation of God in Jesus Christ should be accepted as a miracle wrought by God and by God alone. Only the apostles and evangelists of the early Church, behind whom lay the age-long discipline of these two commandments, could rightly understand and accept the divine authority to which Jesus laid claim, because they had grasped that absolute distinction between God and humanity which the Old Testament teaches. Where other religions held sway, it would have been quite easy, and would have caused no offence, to ascribe divinity to Jesus Christ, as divinity is understood in the myths of those religions. There one of the features that recurs most constantly is the raising of a human to the level of a god. But if people have become accustomed to stretch out their hands and take something—in this case deity—to themselves, they are no longer able and willing to regard it as something that they can receive from God's hand, as the gift of God alone.

4

God's Will as Made Manifest in Law

The Ten Commandments are so important that it was right and natural to concentrate first on them. But actually they form only a small part of that rich collection of laws in which the righteous will of God for the ordering of his people finds expression in the Old Testament. Now at this point we touch one of those areas of the Old Testament in which even the most faithful readers of the Bible find it difficult to feel themselves at home. So before we come to the laws of conduct themselves, we must note a few points that are necessary for an understanding of the form in which the laws have come down to us.

The various single precepts and laws have been grouped together in a number of collections for the most part without any clear principle of organization or arrangement. The oldest of these collections is that which has commonly come to be called the Book of the Covenant, Exodus 21–23. A later collection is to be found in Deuteronomy 12–26 [the so-called Deuteronomic Code], and another in the so-called Holiness Code in Leviticus 17–26. But we must not imagine that because certain laws are found only in later collections they are necessarily of later origin than the laws found in other collections. Two questions have to be kept quite distinct. One is that of the process by which various laws were brought together in the collections. The other is that of the period in which these individual laws originated.

Deciding Cases

In ancient Israel, declaration of judgment was normally made at the gate of the city. In Ruth 4 we find a picturesque description, showing how few were the conditions that had to be fulfilled for the gathering of an assembly in which justice could be done. The plaintiff went to the gate of the city, probably the only open space available, called together the elders, and then proceedings could begin. There was, then, no professional class of judges; those who gave judgment were lay folk, in particular the elders among the people (see also Jer 26:10). Here decisions were given as to all those legal questions that are likely to arise in a small community; questions of family law, loans and security, liability for injuries, laws governing slaves, laws for the protection of the poor; and, further, such matters as offences against property, and even violence and murder. Now what were the basic principles, in accordance with which decisions had to be taken? These are set forth for us in conditional form, in sentences beginning with the word "if." A number of good examples appear in the Book of the Covenant—Exodus 22:1–15: "If someone steals an ox . . . ," "If a thief is found breaking in . . . ," etc. But these "ifs" are not just hypothetical; they refer to cases that might actually occur.

As far as such legal formulas are concerned, there is not very much difference between Israel and other peoples of the ancient Near East. We may even suppose that the nomadic tribes of Israel, when they entered Canaan, took over a good deal of the legal tradition that they found already existing in the cities of Canaan. Now that they had adopted a settled way of living instead of the nomadic life of the desert, they were face to face with entirely different conditions and a large number of new problems; they had no developed code of law to cover all the cases that might arise. It is thus that we are able to explain the fact that Israel's ancient codes of law have so many points in common with the traditions of law that were current throughout the whole of the Near East in that period.[1]

This tradition of law, as we said, existed in Canaan at the time when the Israelites entered it; but it must not be supposed that Israel just took it over in a lump without examination. From this ancient body of law, based on experience and checked and refined through many centuries, Israel made its own selection; and, as we can clearly see, at many points made changes in it, in order to bring it into line with its own understanding of law and its own faith.

---

1. The best known of these other collections of laws is the so-called Code of Hammurabi, the collection of laws of the Babylonian King Hammurabi carved on a great block of stone, the discovery of which in 1901–2 caused great excitement at the time. [Ed.] See online: www.kchanson.com/ANCDOCS/meso/hammurabi.html. For a translation with notes, see Richardson, *Hammurabi's Laws*; and Roth, "The Laws of Hammurabi."

But the decisions given by the lay judges at the gate of the city were not decisions against which there could be no appeal. From time to time cases arose which were too difficult to be decided by the elders in the gate. For these, too, provision was made:

> If a judicial decision is too difficult for you to make between one kind of bloodshed and another, one kind of legal right and another, or one kind of assault and another—any such matters of dispute in your towns—then you shall immediately go up to the place that Yahweh your God will choose, where you shall consult with the levitical priests and the judge who is in office in those days; they shall announce to you the decision in the case. Carry out exactly the decision that they announce to you from the place that Yahweh will choose, diligently observing everything they instruct you. You must carry out fully the law that they interpret for you or the ruling that they announce to you; do not turn aside from the decision that they announce to you, either to the right or to the left. (Deut 17:8–11)

Thus it was possible for the local judges to seek guidance and direction at the sanctuary and from the priests.[2] For we must not imagine the priests in those days to have been entirely occupied with the duties of worship—the sacrifices and offerings of the shrine. The priests' maintenance and passing on of that law of God that had been entrusted to their care was almost more important than their service at the altar. They were in possession of the ancient revealed declarations of the will of God. These constituted a body

2. [Ed.] On Deuteronomy 17, see von Rad, *Deuteronomy*, 117–20.

of sacred knowledge of which the priests were guardians, a treasury out of which, on the high feast days of the people, they proclaimed in the name of God the rules which were binding upon them for the ordering of their lives. Of these rules we have already spoken; they were in fact, in one form or another, the Ten Commandments.

We find similar declarations in the Book of the Covenant also. One such list of declarations is to be found in Exodus 21:12–17 (quoted here in modified order):

> Whoever strikes a person mortally shall be put to death.
>
> Whoever strikes father or mother shall be put to death.
>
> Whoever curses father or mother shall be put to death.
>
> Whoever kidnaps a person, whether that person is sold or is still held in possession, shall be put to death.

A third list of commandments of this kind is to be found in Deuteronomy 27:15–26.[3] We shall come back to these later on (pp. 59–62). The difference between these declarations and the formulation of the law of the village is at once clear. These are not conditional in form, or set out at length with minute attention to detail; they are declaratory in character, as concise and as weighty as could be. These demands are unconditional—and this point is made even clearer in the Ten Commandments by the personal form of the address— God who is "I" speaks to a person who is "thou." In a word, this is the law of God as immediately revealed, and in these

---

3. [Ed.] On Deuteronomy 27, see von Rad, *Deuteronomy*, 164–69.

commandments we come to the basic rock of the revelation of the will of God for us, as that was imparted to Moses.

We thus see that, in the early history of Israel, we encounter two kinds of law, and that these are markedly different from one another. It is not altogether easy to see in what sense the term "the law of God" can be applied to both these forms of law. The conditional "law of the gate," to the practice of which Israel became accustomed only after it had entered into the land of Canaan, was based generally on the understanding of law of the Near Eastern peoples with their manifold experiences. Yet, true as this is, the Old Testament makes no theological distinction between the declaratory law of God as proclaimed at the sanctuary and the conditional law as practiced "at the gate." The claim of each to be divine revelation is recognized. In spite of the origin of this second kind of law in the experience of nations outside Israel, Israel was prepared here also to hear the voice of its God speaking directly to his people. What other course was open to them? If all law that is an expression of justice and mercy has its origin in God, then this kind of law also must possess the authority of a direct revelation from God. So, when the books of the law came to be compiled, the utterances of the "law of the gate" were combined with the declarations of the law of God as recorded in the tradition of the priests and of Moses. From the point of view of theology, no difference was made between them; they are placed on exactly the same level.[4]

4. [Ed.] See von Rad, *Old Testament Theology*, vol. 1, 189–203.

The Call to Holiness

We shall now go on to consider rather more in detail the contents of this revelation of the will of God. Once more we must recall that, over all this multitude of commands, regulations and ordinances, stands the authority of the First Commandment (see pp. 28–37). And we must also bear in mind one other great commandment, so comprehensive and so concise that it may be taken as a-summary of the many particular commands: "You shall be holy; for I Yahweh your God am holy" (Lev 19:2).

The reader of the Bible at first finds the number and variety of the commandments confusing. But this very variety reminds us of the principle that God's righteous will is to be brought to bear on every aspect of life. There is to be no area, either of public or of private life, over which the sovereign authority of God is not proclaimed. In relation to every aspect of man's existence and man's activity, this claim of God to sovereignty is set forth as the most urgent concern of all. The basis for all life of men in community is law. We have already mentioned that Israel had in old times its tried and tested standards of right and wrong, in the light of which judgment was pronounced "in the gate." But we find also another set of commandments, which tell us in a much more personal way that the judge must at every point be subject to the will of God:

> You shall not utter a false report. You shall not join hands with a wicked man, to be a malicious witness. You shall not follow a multitude to do evil; nor shall you bear witness in a suit, turning aside after a multitude, so as to pervert justice; nor shall you be partial to a poor man in his suit

> . . . You shall not pervert the justice due to your
> poor in his suit. Keep far from a false charge,
> and do not slay the innocent and righteous, for I
> will not acquit the wicked. And you shall take no
> bribe, for a bribe blinds the officials, and subverts
> the cause of those who are in the right. You shall
> not oppress a stranger; you know the heart of a
> stranger, for you were strangers in the land of
> Egypt. (Exod 23:1–9)

It is the entirely personal character of these rules that
gives them their strictly binding character. There is an "I,"
who speaks ("I will not acquit the wicked"), and there is
a "thou" to whom this "I" speaks in the most direct and
personal fashion. When commands are given in this form,
there is no possibility of evading them. The administration
of justice is here represented as something in which God is
personally and very deeply interested. He speaks directly
about it; he sets forth a claim, which demands obedience
not in general, but in the quite definite terms of a particular
situation.

In this "mirror for magistrates," one thing that strikes
us with special force is the care and concern expressed for
the poor and the stranger, that is, for the lower ranks in society. This is a thread that runs through the whole of the Old
Testament tradition; the commandments give expression to
a concern for the poor that finds no parallel elsewhere. Let
us listen to the regulations concerning loans and pledges:

> If ever you take your neighbor's garment in
> pledge, you shall restore it to him before the sun
> goes down; for that is his only covering, it is his
> mantle for his body; in what else shall he sleep?

> And if he cries to me, I will hear, for I am com-
> passionate. (Exod 22:26–27)

> When you make your neighbor a loan of any
> sort, you shall not go into his house to fetch his
> pledge. You shall stand outside, and the man to
> whom you make the loan shall bring the pledge
> out to you. (Deut 24:10–11)

Or here is the law of interest:

> If you lend money to any of my people with you
> who is poor, you shall not be to him as a creditor,
> and you shall not exact interest from him. (Exod
> 22:25)

Again and again these regulations come back to the
subject of the poor; in every possible way they try to make
his lot easier and protect him against extortion:

> You shall not oppress a hired servant who is poor
> and needy, whether he is one of your brethren
> or one of the sojourners who are in your land
> within your towns; you shall give him his hire
> on the day he earns it, before the sun goes down
> (for he is poor, and sets his heart upon it); lest he
> cry against you to Yahweh, and it be sin in you.
> (Deut 24:14–15)

To hear these commands is to recognize that they lay
claim to the whole man, to man in his entirety. The evidence does not support the idea that the law of Moses is
content with an outward obedience, and that Jesus was the
first to transfer the problem of obedience to the world of
thought and motive. We have only to think of such commandments as the following:

> You shall not hate your brother in your heart,
> but you shall reason with your neighbor, lest
> you bear sin because of him. You shall not take
> vengeance or bear any grudge against the sons of
> your own people, but you shall love your neigh-
> bor as yourself: I am Yahweh. (Lev 19:17–18)

We feel a deep and instinctive sympathy with these detailed laws for society; they sound almost up-to-date! Do we not find already expressed in them all the ideals that were the inspiration of the great social movements of the last century? Yes. But what matters is that we should recognize the vital difference between the Old Testament and the approach of much modern "Social Christianity."

All these modern social movements take people as their starting-point; they think in terms of people's claims to happiness, or of human dignity, or of the infinite value of the individual soul; the same general idea can be expressed in a great number of different ways. But in the entire Old Testament there is not a word about any of these things; the one and only thing the Old Testament is concerned about is the will of God. The law must not be broken, and the poor must not be oppressed; but this is not because a person is so valuable and has so many justifiable claims on life; it is because such things are contrary to God's will. And this righteous will of God is binding on a person and cannot be evaded. The basic assumption on which the whole Old Testament rests is that person belongs to God, and that the first and foremost of his tasks is to serve God and obey him.

The Sabbath

In this connection we must say something also about the law requiring that the seventh day is to be kept holy (Exod 20:8–11). It is remarkable that the Sabbath, in the Old Testament, is not understood as the day on which some special service of worship is held. We hear nothing of any special religious practices from which the special importance of the Sabbath day might be derived. No, the Sabbath day is the day of rest; for rest it has been appointed and for nothing else. But this is not the rest that a man might permit himself from time to time, proportioned to the work that he has accomplished. It is a cessation of work that is imposed on man from outside, by God himself. Modern people may well find strange the idea that simply doing no work can honor God. But the ancient people regarded work not as something holy in itself, but rather as something that can set up a wall of separation between even God and humans. We sometimes feel that the duty to work has unquestioned sovereignty over people; but this rest that is imposed upon people from without denies the exclusive claim that work would sometimes make.

The Sabbath has sometimes been called "a sacrifice of rest," and indeed the term is not inappropriate. But the Sabbath could also be described as the normal day. It is the day that a person does not fill to the full with one's own ordinary employments, but which one gives back to God clean and unused. Thereby one returns to a truer order, the order that God appointed for the world at the time of the creation. God, so we are told, rested after the creation, and by so doing he made rest itself a holy thing. "Upon the whole course of the world's history rests like a benediction God's repose on the seventh day of creation, which knows no evening," says one modern writer. But, if one no longer pays attention to this rest, one's life falls victim to all manner of slavery.

Very similar ideas underlie the ordinance that lays down that the seventh year is to be observed as a year of Sabbath:

> When you enter the land that I am giving you, the land shall observe a sabbath for Yahweh. Six years you shall sow your field, and six years you shall prune your vineyard, and gather in their yield; but in the seventh year there shall be a sabbath of complete rest for the land, a sabbath to Yahweh; you shall not sow your field or prune your vineyard. (Lev 25:2–4)

So the subject here is a period of hallowed rest, of lying fallow, for the soil, which is to be proclaimed at the end of every six years. Earlier we have referred to the Feast of Tabernacles, which was celebrated as a festival of the renewal of the covenant of the people with God. On that occasion God caused his sovereignty over people to be proclaimed anew. But once every seven years, the festival of the renewal of the covenant was accompanied by another special usage— the proclamation of the year of Sabbath. We learn what its purpose was from what may be regarded as one of the most fundamental of all the laws in the Old Testament:

> The land shall not be sold in perpetuity, for the land is mine; with me you are but aliens and tenants. (Lev 25:23)

God is the true owner of the land![5] It is he who grants it to humans for their use. The purpose of the year of

5 [Ed.] See Habel, *The Land Is Mine*; and Brueggemann, *The Land*.

Sabbath is to drive this truth firmly home into the mind of the people. Humans think that they can treat the land as their own possession; they grasp at all the mysterious powers of the fertile soil, at the treasures of the earth, and they forget God, who gave all this to them. They regard the land as their own domain, which they can exploit in all directions exactly as they please. They can buy the land and sell it; they can let it for a longer or shorter period, exactly as circumstances demand. But over against people's arbitrary assertion of their claim to possession of the land, God sets up his claim to be the true owner of it.

There can be no doubt that in the early periods of Israel's history the command concerning the year of Sabbath was really obeyed and carried out. In the course of years some grow poor and fall into debt; others grow richer; and thus the true economic relationship between the people is perverted and falls into confusion. But it is not the will of God that these changes should last forever: land and soil are not to be permanently sold. At the end of every six years, Israel must pause and draw back the hand that they had stretched out to assert their claim to full ownership of the land. By doing so, they bear outward and visible witness to the truth that God alone and no other is the true owner of the land. At the end of the year, in a solemn religious ceremony, lots are cast anew to determine human occupation of the land.

In the ancient era of the patriarchs, and at the time when Israel was mainly a country of peasants, it was possible to put the command concerning the year of Sabbath into effect. But in ancient Israel, as sooner or later in every other nation of the world, the old peasant economy of barter and exchange gradually changes into an economy based primarily on money. The cultural life of the people comes to be concentrated in the towns. Alongside the free peasant living on his fields we meet the townsman who lives by trade. When the economic situation has so completely changed, what is to be done about keeping the commandment of the Sabbath year? How is it possible to make it in any way applicable to the towns, which have now fully passed into the stage of the money economy? We find the answer to this question in another form of the law governing the year of Sabbath,[6] which clearly corresponds to this later situation:

> Every seven years you shall grant a remission of debts. And this is the manner of the remission: every creditor shall remit the claim that is held against a neighbor; not exacting it of a neighbor who is a member of the community, because Yahweh's remission has been proclaimed. (Deut 15:1–2)

This new way of expressing the law of the Sabbath year is a good example of the way in which the laws can be modified and adapted to changed situations. A law is originally suited to one level of economic and cultural life. Then the conditions to which it was directed change. The law is not given up. It is adapted to the situation that now exists, and it is proclaimed afresh in relation to these new conditions. A command given by God cannot fall to the ground. It is not tied just to one particular level of cultural development; once revealed, it has permanent and unchangeable authority over humanity, however widely the conditions and manner of their life may change. And yet the law has

6. [Ed.] See von Rad, *Deuteronomy*, 105–7.

not remained completely unchanged in its application to new circumstances.

God's Will and the Human Heart

In its new form, it is not so much a proclamation of the sovereign rights of God as an admonition to brotherly love. But what gives it authority is, above all else, its demand, not for mere outward observance, but for full inner compliance with the will of God. The one who speaks to humans demands the whole human heart, and tests the most hidden and secret impulses of his inner being.

> Be careful that you do not entertain a mean thought thinking, "The seventh year, the year of remission is near," and therefore view your needy neighbor with hostility and give nothing; your neighbor might cry to Yahweh against you, and you would incur guilt. Give liberally and be ungrudging when you do so, for on this account Yahweh your God will bless you in all your work and in all that you undertake. (Deut 15:9–10)

In Deuteronomy we find a list of prohibitions, in which this claim of God upon human life, even to the most hidden nooks and crannies of his being, is most impressively set forth:

> Cursed be anyone who makes an idol or casts an image, anything abhorrent to Yahweh, the work of an artisan, and sets it up in secret. All the people shall respond, saying, "Amen."
> Cursed be anyone who dishonors father or mother. All the people shall say, "Amen."

> Cursed be anyone who moves his neighbor's boundary mark. All the people shall say, "Amen."
>
> Cursed be anyone who misleads a blind person on the road. All the people shall say, "Amen."
>
> Cursed be anyone who deprives the alien, the orphan, and the widow of justice. All the people shall say, "Amen."
>
> Cursed be anyone who lies with his father's wife . . . All the people shall say, "Amen."
>
> Cursed be anyone who lies with any kind of beast . . . All the people shall say, "Amen."
>
> Cursed be anyone who lies with his sister . . . All the people shall say, "Amen."
>
> Cursed be anyone who lies with his mother-in-law. And all the people shall say, "Amen."
>
> Cursed be anyone who strikes down a neighbor in secret. And all the people shall say, "Amen."
>
> Cursed be anyone who takes a bribe to shed innocent blood. And all the people shall say, "Amen."
>
> Cursed by anyone who does not uphold the words of this law by observing them. And all the people shall say, "Amen." (Deut 27:15–26)

Clearly the form of these verses is liturgical.[7] The priests set forth the commands; the people answer and give assent to them. It is probable that the recital of this list of commandments was one of the high points in that ceremony of the renewal of the covenant that took place at the Feast of Tabernacles. If we read the list again, we shall note that the prohibitions deal with a whole series of different subjects, but that they almost all have one thing in

7. [Ed.] See von Rad, *Deuteronomy*, 164–69.

common. They deal with the kind of offences that a person is liable to commit in secret. An idol set up and worshipped in secret—we have already referred to this—who has any knowledge of the fact? A neighbor's boundary stone removed at night; failure to pay the respect due to parents; the meanness of leading a blind man astray—who sees all this? What tribunal is there that takes note of such offences as these? And then the whole wide field of sexual relationships! What proportion of the offences committed in this field ever comes before an earthly judge? What is so splendid is that the people of the Old Testament recognize that God has set forth commandments that apply to those areas in which one is not acting under the eyes of one's fellows or in the full light of day. There are many areas of life, which the arm of earthly law and justice is too short to reach, or with which perhaps such law is incompetent to deal. But none of these areas escapes the watchful eyes of God, and the people are called to recognize that he exercises his righteous judgment even over that which is hidden from the eyes of others. The language of the list of commands that we have quoted is made particularly stern, lest one might mistakenly imagine that in these areas of life one is less exposed than in others to the eyes of God the righteous judge.

Let us look back once again on these laws that we have quoted and briefly explained. Two immediate impressions are likely to remain deeply stamped upon our minds.

The first is that these laws take the earth so seriously— those things that happen in the realm of time and space. Here is a will of God for the life of humanity upon earth, a will that permits of no evasion. God speaks directly to all the levels and all the aspects of human life, and here, upon this earth, he demands the obedience of humans without delay and without argument.

The second point is the strength of God's will for fellowship among people. His purpose is to establish among people a fellowship based on his commandments and ordered according to his will. For the earth and the people on it alike belong to God. The first verse of Psalm 24 sounds rather like a comprehensive conclusion drawn from God's self-revelation in the laws:

> The earth is Yahweh's and all that is in it,
>> the world, and those who live in it. (Ps 24:1)

This is the central purpose of the commandments. Their aim is to bring humanity back into obedience to God. Humans belong to God; they must be willing to dedicate themselves to God's service; they should be most closely linked to him in thanksgiving and worship. More than this; this Old Testament people is told in the plainest terms that what this God requires of it is the deepest and purest love: "You shall love Yahweh your God with all your heart, and with all your soul, and with all your might" (Deut 6:5). Jesus himself affirms that this is the greatest of all the commandments (Mark 12:29); and that there is a second like to it: "you shall love your neighbor as yourself" (Lev 19:18).

The Commandments as Expressions of God's Gracious Will

How did the people of the old covenant regard this revelation of the will of God? How did those, to whom it was first and particularly addressed, think of it? To this important question the answer is surprisingly clear and free from ambiguity, and it is likely to upset completely the idea that many Christians have formed of "law" in the Old Testament. For what we hear on every side is the expression of amazement and thankfulness for the marvel of this revelation of the will of God. "He has caused us to know his mighty righteousness and his judgments." This is the keynote, which sounds again and again, as men bear witness to their response to the revelation of God.

The commandments are regarded as an expression of God's gracious will; they are the absolutely reliable guarantee that God desires to have this people as his own. It is he who has given these ordinances to the people. For what purpose can he have given them, other than that the people should live in the light of his countenance? The picture of the law that we find in the Old Testament as a whole is not that it is a heavy burden to people, or that it turns life into weariness. On the contrary; Psalm 119 and Psalm 19:7–13 give us some idea of the passionate thankfulness and happiness with which the people of God in the Old Testament received the Law from the hand of God. In those two psalms we find expressed again and again the thought that in this revelation of the will of God true life, life in the presence of God, is being offered to people. For, if God has undertaken to order a community and to develop it according to his will, surely in that community it is the true human life that is coming to expression. Moses's speech of farewell in Deuteronomy at its close comes back to this point with concentrated emphasis:

> so they [your children] may diligently observe all
> the words of this law. This is no trifling matter for
> you, but rather your very life. (Deut 32:46–47)

"Your very life." This needs a little fuller exposition. According to the testimony of the Bible, life is something very different from that which we generally suppose. Life is not simply a mysterious power, which is part of the being of this world; something which people possess, which is holy in itself, and follows its own internal laws. Life is a gift that comes from the hand of God alone. Life belongs to God; and people possess life—this is the point that may strike us as strange and unexpected—only when one is living in accordance with the will of God. Life in disobedience is, in the eyes of God, life that has been forfeited. Let us once more pay attention to the way in which Moses in his farewell discourse speaks of life:

> See, I have set before you this day life and prosperity, death and adversity. If you obey the commandments of Yahweh your God that I am commanding you today, by loving Yahweh your God, walking in his ways . . . God will bless you . . . But if your heart turns away and you do not hear, but are led astray to bow down to other gods and serve them, I declare to you today that you shall perish; you shall not live long in the land that you are crossing over the Jordan to enter and possess. I call heaven and earth to witness against you today that I have set before you life and death, blessings and curses. Choose life so that you and your descendants may live. (Deut 30:15–19)

How strange is the way in which Moses here speaks of life and death![8] He does not speak as though life and death were things that already "belonged" to the hearers, as though each was already theirs as part of human destiny, as though they were people who were now standing roughly half way between the beginning of life and its end. No, they are addressed as people who, through hearing the word of God, have for the first time been brought to the point where they can make a decisive choice between life and death.

This would perhaps be the right point at which to end our chapter. For this is the decisive word of the Old Testament concerning the commandments of God: that in them life is offered to people, and that they are a manifestation of the gracious will of God towards people.

A New Relationship

The people of the old covenant were very well aware of human incapacity and of humanity's refusal to live in obedience to the revelation of God's will. In the books of the prophets there is hardly a chapter in which a bitter outcry is not raised against the disobedience and the obstinacy of people. Yet to these people, who in their own day were fated to see and to proclaim God's unqualified verdict of condemnation upon people, the bright promise was given that the time was not far off when God himself would rise up, to bridge the gulf and to heal the bitter opposition that had arisen between God and humanity. They foretold that God himself would bring a new person into existence:

8. von Rad, *Deuteronomy*, 184–85.

> A new heart I will give you, and a new spirit I
> will put within you; and I will remove from your
> body the heart of stone and give you a heart of
> flesh. I will put my spirit within you, and make
> you follow my statutes and be careful to observe
> my ordinances. (Ezek 36:26–27)

Now note that here too reference is made to the commandments. But the theme of this prophecy is that, through the miracle of a rebirth from on high, God will make human hearts readily obedient to the commandments, and will turn them back again to the will of God as he has revealed it. Jeremiah foretells this miracle even more clearly:

> The days are surely coming, says Yahweh, when
> I will make a new covenant with the house of
> Israel and the house of Judah . . . But this is the
> covenant that I will make with the house of Israel
> after those days, says Yahweh: I will put my law
> within them, and I will write it on their hearts;
> and I will be their God, and they shall be my peo-
> ple. No longer shall they teach one another, or
> say to each other, "Know Yahweh," for they shall
> all know me, from the least of them to the great-
> est, says Yahweh; for I will forgive their iniquity,
> and remember their sin no more. (Jer 31:31–34)

This famous passage has often been misunderstood.[9] There is nothing in it to suggest that, when the new covenant is given, the revelation of God given under the old covenant is no longer valid. How could God withdraw a revelation of his will that he has once given? But under the new covenant the relationship of people to the commandments will not

9. [Ed.] See Brueggemann, *A Commentary on Jeremiah*, 291–95.

be the same as it had been under the old. No longer will the commandments be proclaimed to humanity from without; no longer will they be imposed upon them as a will other than their own and bring them into condemnation. Then everyone will bear the commandments of God in their own hearts and will find that God's will is their own will as well.

Jesus Christ, on the night on which he was betrayed, reminded his disciples about this passage from the prophet Jeremiah and spoke of the new covenant that was to be sealed with his blood. He it was who had completely made his own heart and will one with the will of God; it was in him and in his perfect obedience that the new covenant, the new fellowship with God, was made available to us. As Paul says, he is "the firstborn within a large family" (Rom 8:29).

As long as this world lasts, our new life in Christ is "hidden with Christ in God" (Col 3:3). We still live the life of a body and of a will that have not yet been completely set free from the slavery of sin. And so the commandments of the Old Testament have still their importance for us as guardians and as guides. But they can never take from us that fellowship with God that has been given to us in Christ; they can never again become a law that brings us into condemnation.

5

From Promise to Fulfillment

From Genesis to Joshua

The stories about Moses in the Old Testament form only one part of one great book, which begins with the book of Genesis and runs through to the end of the book of Joshua and the occupation of the land of Canaan by Israel.[1] This book comprises an immense mass of material running from the creation of the world up to Israel's entry into Canaan; and later it was found to be a matter of sheer practical necessity to break up the one large book into a number of main divisions. Now, if we are to understand the stories about Moses, we must be familiar with this book as a whole, with the great general structure that makes up its unity.

If we look at the contents of this book, we are likely to find them distinctly odd—from the creation of the world

1. [Ed.] Von Rad's treatment of Genesis to Joshua (known as the "Hexateuch" [six books]) he treats in "The Problem of the Hexateuch," in *From Genesis to Chronicles*, 1–58; see also von Rad, *Old Testament Theology*, vol. 1, 129–35.

to the occupation of Canaan by Israel! What a magnificent opening—and what an unimpressive conclusion! So great a journey to such an insignificant end! And what an expenditure of divine guidance, miracles, and judgments! On the human side, what an expenditure of exaltation and humiliation, of obedience and rebellion, all leading up to this trivial goal!

And yet here is the meaning of the whole story. It shows how God has been secretly constructing a way of blessing and salvation in a world that has separated itself from him. The turning point of the whole story is where it passes over from the general history of the human race to the story of one particular process of redemption. And here, at this point, is recorded the word of God to Abraham, in which the whole of the future is summed up: "I will bless you . . . and in you all the families of the earth will be blessed" (Gen 12:2–3). Here, at the very beginning of the Old Testament history of salvation something is said about its end: already we are told that God's plan of salvation will broaden out from the particular to the universal, and that in the end it will be significant for humanity as a whole far beyond the limits of Israel. It is only in this context that we can understand why Israel's entry into Canaan is so important.

We may find it strange that God should single out one country and should concentrate his purposes within it. But the Bible deals in terms of God's will for this visible world, and his choice of the land of Canaan is an essential part of that will. The most universal and most spiritual of all the prophets of the Old Testament is Second Isaiah;[2] yet we

2. [Ed.] "Second Isaiah" refers to the material in Isaiah 40–55. For

must not forget that even here the whole emphasis of his prophecy falls once again upon the land. The exiled people are to return again to the promised land—here is the heart of his message (Isa 49:14–21; 52:7–12; 54). So this return is not to be understood primarily as something that takes place in the world of thought, as something that we might call a religious renewal of humanity. The promise that is given to Israel is not in the first place a promise that they shall have a new relationship with God. And yet this changed relationship does go along with the other promise, the promise of the land.[3] It seems that God wanted to base his claim on man, and his promise to man, on the very deepest foundation of human existence—and that is the earth on which we live. From this follow all the deep conflicts between people and the claim that God in these terms makes upon them. It follows that the work of God upon people is to be carried out in an area in which conflict between God and people cannot possibly be avoided. When God chose this land of Canaan as his own, he also chose the place called Golgotha, which is a part of it—and this means something far more than a piece of geographical information.

This one tremendous book (Genesis to Joshua) is, if we look at its contents, constructed on the general plan of Promise–Fulfillment. The time of the patriarchs is the time of promise; the occupation of Canaan under Joshua is the time of fulfillment. So the road from Egypt through

von Rad's extended treatment of Second Isaiah, see *Old Testament Theology*, vol. 2, 238–62; see also Brueggemann, *Hopeful Imagination*, 89–130.

3. [Ed.] See von Rad, "The Promised Land and Yahweh's Land in the Hexateuch," in *From Genesis to Chronicles*, 58–68; and Brueggemann, *The Land*.

the wilderness to Canaan is the road that the people must follow from promise to fulfillment; and in all the various records of the wanderings we are being shown, in typical form, things that are true also of the road that the people of God in the New Testament has to tread from promise to fulfillment. That road towards fulfillment, on which the Church of Jesus Christ upon earth is moving, casts, as it were, its shadow (Heb 8:5) backwards upon that earlier road.[4] Here are crises of distress and acts of divine deliverance that may recur again and again in our experience too, so long as it is ours to walk by faith and not by sight.

Wandering in the Wilderness

As early as the period of the prophets, the time that Israel spent in the wilderness had come to be regarded as the period in which the true relationship between God and his people had been visible in its purest and most original form.[5] Israel in the wilderness had not yet entered into the corrupting environment of the higher civilization of Canaan. It was not in a position to run after other nations in order to insure its safety by alliances with them. In all its times of need it was thrown back upon God and upon God alone; in that "land of drought and deep darkness . . . a land that none passes through" (Jer 2:6; see also Hos 13:5), it was to the guidance of God and to nothing else that they must look. In the wilderness there was nothing that could create

4. [Ed.] On the relationship between the testaments, see von Rad, *Old Testament Theology*, vol. 2, 319–409.

5. [Ed.] On the Wilderness Wandering traditions, see von Rad, *Old Testament Theology*, vol. 1, 280–89.

a barrier between the people and its Lord. They must put their trust in God alone for the supply of every need, beginning with the need for daily bread. It is for this reason that all these stories of the needs of the ancient people and of the promises made to them foreshadow almost exactly the experiences of the new people of God, the Church. Of one of these stories Paul writes, "These things happened to them to serve as an example,[6] and they were written down to instruct us, on whom the ends of the ages have come" (1 Cor 10:11).

Let us look for a moment at the story of the manna (Exodus 16), and especially at the second part of it (from v. 16 on). It is clear that the narrator is not just telling us of a strange occurence that took place in the earliest days of Israel's history. The event that is recorded belongs to one particular time and place; but at the same time it is typical, that is, it shows forth something that is true at all times and in all places.

When the manna had fallen, the people went out to gather it; and then they found that each had gathered just enough for the needs of himself and of his family. They had gone out to gather quite freely, "some more, some less," and yet, when all was in, there was neither too little nor too much. Here is expressed the consoling thought that God gives to everyone their own; God will provide for each exactly that which they need in their particular situation. But there is another important point in the story; the manna cannot be kept. Some tried to store it up, but it went bad in their hands. We cannot arbitrarily lay claim to more than

6. In the Greek, "typically"—as a "type" or foreshadowing of something yet to come. [Ed.] See von Rad, "Typological Interpretation of the Old Testament."

that which God is pleased to give us. We must be willing to receive it from his hand day by day. If we are dealing with God, the only way in which it is possible to live is "from hand to mouth."

In the interpretation of the miracle of the manna in the book of Deuteronomy, the spiritual aspect is even more strongly stressed:

> Remember the long way Yahweh your God has led you these forty years in the wilderness . . . He humbled you by letting you hunger, then by feeding you with manna, with which neither you nor ancestors were acquainted, in order to make you understand that one does not live by bread alone, but by every word that come from the mouth of Yahweh. (Deut 8:2–3)

According to this passage the manna was not food just for the body; it was given, rather, in order to show people that food for the body is not enough.[7] People can truly live only when God gives them the gift of his own word.

Spying out the Land

The continuity of the narrative of the Israel's wanderings in the wilderness, as we have it today, is sharply interrupted by the story of the spies, who were sent to spy out the land of Canaan (Numbers 13–14). This story gives us the answer to the question why the chosen people did not follow the shortest route (from south to north) in order to take possession of the promised land, and why one whole generation of adults was condemned to die out in the wilderness

7. [Ed.] On this passage, see von Rad, *Deuteronomy*, 71–72.

after long wanderings hither and thither, without having seen the fulfillment of the promise. The report that the spies bring back is self-contradictory. The land is very fair (Num 13:27; 14:7); but how can Israel take possession of it? The difficulties are too great to be overcome. Thus they were unfaithful witnesses concerning the gift that God had promised to give his people. For the moment the people fell under the evil influence of their little faith.

Faced by the splendor of God's plan for them, they fall into a panic. Now they see clearly what they have let themselves in for, and they wish to retreat, because they are not able to put their full confidence in God. They see that the task before them is by all human standards impossible, and they completely lose heart. They go so far as to think of choosing for themselves another captain, who shall lead them back to Egypt (Num 14:4). And what is involved in such proposals is nothing less than the abandonment and the betrayal of the whole series of saving acts that God has performed for them, and those that he has promised still to do for them. Only Joshua and Caleb are prepared to condemn this unbelief: "If Yahweh is pleased with us, he will bring us into this land and give it to us, a land which flows with milk and honey. Only, do not rebel against Yahweh . . . Yahweh is with us" (Num 14:8–9).

The people are prepared to go so far as to threaten to stone these two men, who alone have honored God by putting their trust in his word. But then God rises up to judgment (14:10–11), for it is God himself whom the people have blasphemed. Moses prays for the people, and God's answer to the prayer of Moses is most remarkable. The unbelief of this whole generation is immeasurably deep; yet even this cannot prevent the fulfillment of God's purposes of salvation. The failure of this generation cannot frustrate God's plan at some future date to reveal his salvation to the whole world: "As I live . . . all the earth shall be filled with the glory of Yahweh" (Num 14:21).

But this generation cannot enter into the promised land. And what now follows is strange and unexpected. The people had pretended that it was out of concern for the well-being of their children that they had decided to be disobedient to the calling of God and to return to Egypt (14:3); and now it is decreed that they shall die in the wilderness, but that their children shall be heirs of the promise (14:31)! When this announcement is made, the pride of the people is touched. What they would not trust God to give them they are now going to take by their own efforts. They will take the land in possession by their own strength. It is in vain that Moses warns them: "Yahweh will not be with you."

> But they presumed to go up to the heights of the hill country, even though the ark of the covenant of Yahweh, and Moses, had not left the camp. Then the Amalekites and the Canaanites who lived in that hill country came down and defeated them, pursuing them as far as Hormah. (Num 14:44–45)

So for many years the Israelites wandered in the wilderness. At last the time arrives when, according to the word of the Lord, they are to be allowed to go forward and to enter on their inheritance in Canaan.

Balak and Balaam

At this point in the narrative occurs the remarkable history of Balaam and his attempt to curse the people. In a wonderful way, this story sums up the whole of the revelation of the purpose of God given through Moses. So, as the conclusion of our study, we will look rather closely at this story and its inner meaning (Numbers 22–24).[8]

The people of Israel are now encamped "in the plains of Moab beyond the Jordan at Jericho." They are just at the point of entry on the fulfillment of the promise; and precisely at this moment they are threatened by a danger more serious than any to which they have previously been exposed.

The story begins by setting forth in very strong terms the fear and terror of Balak, king of Moab, at the arrival of this invading army. He wishes to protect himself against folk whom he regards as barbarian disturbers of the peace. But he does not follow what would seem to us to be the obvious course; he does not take up arms against them, he does not set in motion against them any measures of outward violence. He sends messengers to Balaam the diviner: "Come now, curse this people for me, since they are too mighty for me."

As the ancient world looked at things, a curse was very much more than an evil word. The one who curses sets in motion those demonic powers by which the human world is surrounded. It is therefore possible for people to arouse and set in motion these dark powers from the depths, because those powers themselves are possessed by a greedy

8. [Ed.] On Balaam, see von Rad, "The Story of Balaam"; also Hackett, "Balaam"; and Coats, "Balaam: Saint or Sinner?"

and eager desire for the work of destruction; and many people, it was believed, have an uncanny authority over these spirits and the power to command them. Such a one was Balaam, and for that reason he was widely held in repute as a diviner. Balak hopes that with Balaam's help he may be able to strike the people of Israel at the very roots of its existence. But we must carefully note the word "perhaps" in Numbers 22:6: "perhaps I shall be able to defeat them and drive them from the land." Balak regards this as no more than a possibility; when all is said and done, the success of that which he is taking in hand cannot be guaranteed. So on one side there is uncertainty; and, in contrast to it, as our narrative sets it forth, there is something quite sure and certain on the side of God.

On the arrival of Balak's messengers, so we read, Balaam asks for God's counsel—who first forbids him, and then gives him permission to accept the invitation. But we must recognize that Balaam has himself only a dim knowledge of the living God; he turns to his idols—but in such a case as this, what can they do? Although the heathens do not recognize it, it is in reality the living God who guides and rules all things, and so it is to God that the writer immediately directs our attention. In the last resort it was with God that Balaam had to deal.

We must also note, in passing, a difficulty in the literary form in which the narrative is set before us. The story of the meeting of Balaam with the angel of the Lord cannot be exactly the continuation of that which has preceded it. It takes up again the note of warning—God's anger is kindled against Balaam (Num 22:22). In fact, the splendidly told story of Balaam and the she-ass repeats for us in different form and rather more fully that strange meeting of God with Balaam of which we have had one account already in vv. 9–21. In v. 35, we are back at the same point at which we were in v. 20. Balaam is about to set out with the princes of Balak.

Now comes the central and critical point. Balaam has at last seen the angel of the Lord.[9] He does just what any reader would expect him to do—he declares his willingness to go home. But—and this is the most surprising thing of all—that is exactly what he is not to do. Every reader must have been following the course of events with apprehension, for Balaam's purpose is a terrible one—he is setting out to curse the people. If Balaam had at this point been sent home again, the story would have been simply one more edifying tale, showing how God had once again diverted disaster from his people. But God lets the diviner go on his way. He does not bar the road before him; he does not strike him down in his wrath; he will merely direct the word that Balaam is to utter. Here our story gives expression to something that is very important in the faith of the Old Testament; God does not guide history and the destiny of people by continually opposing people in the projects that they have taken in hand. On the contrary, God lets them act. To all appearances, they are acting simply according to their own plans; and yet they cannot avoid becoming the instruments of God and acting in reality according to his plan.

Balaam arrives in the plains of Moab and at once sets to work. Balak leads him up to a mountaintop, and from

9. On the angel of Yahweh, see von Rad, *Old Testament Theology*, vol. 1, 285–89.

there he can see the people encamped in the valley, but only the nearest of them—beyond that his vision cannot reach. At this point of the story the modern reader may find the main interest in the psychological problem; after his encounter with God, what is Balaam's attitude to the work in which he is engaged? But the whole interest of the story, from the point of view of the writer and of the original readers, is concentrated on what Balaam is going to say. Balaam in himself is not now so very important; he is, as it were, a figure of the twilight, and that is as it ought to be. In the sequel we shall see how this famous seer becomes no more than a tool in the hand of God. But the narrative makes one thing perfectly clear to us: Balaam still intends to curse the people and makes all the necessary preparations for doing so.

Balaam has himself led up to a high place; seven altars are set up; sacrifice is offered; and as is customary in such magical rites, he mysteriously changes more than once the place from which he is going to speak. The narrator quite deliberately relates in detail all these magical transactions. The contrast will be all the sharper between this hocus-pocus and the words of blessing that will fall from the lips of Balaam as soon as he begins to speak. The aim of the narrator is to work out this contrast in all its details; this is the central lesson of the whole story. Balaam has ceased to be master of himself. He behaves like an automaton. The purposes of his actions and the results of those actions fall out of any relation to one another. He behaves like a caricature of a man. He is, indeed, serious enough in all that he does. But now that he has set himself against the people of God, he has no control over the effects of his words; indeed he has no control over the words themselves. Where, then, is his ancient fame as a diviner?

In the light of all this, we can well imagine the strained attention with which the reader in ancient times must have awaited the first words that are to fall from Balaam's mouth. And with the very first words the great marvel is revealed. For all his magical practices, Balaam finds himself simply unable to curse:

> How can I curse whom God has not cursed?
> How can I denounce those whom Yahweh
> has not denounced? (Num 23:8)

Here the story of Balaam reaches its culmination. The hidden, inner dimension of all these strange events is now brought out into the open. A prophetic word lays bare that will of God that is hidden from human eyes, that will that is continuously at work in and behind those projects that people may devise for themselves. The blessing of God sets limits on the effect of the darkest and bitterest of curses.

It is a marvelous picture—of Balaam looking down on the people encamped below in total unawareness of what is going on:

> For from the top of the crags I see him,
>   from the hills I behold him;
> Here is a people living alone,
>   and not reckoning itself among the nations!
> (Num 23:9)

This is the way in which the people of the old covenant always thought of itself. In their ancestor Abraham they had been called out from among the company of the peoples. They had been endowed with a special knowledge of God, and with the promise that one day they would be mediators of a salvation that would extend to all the peoples of the earth (Gen 12:3). Thus this people believed that it was God who had set them in a position of isolation from all other peoples. The greatest of its people of God were passionately concerned to keep the treasure of Israel's faith free from all contamination by heathen ideas. At the end of this oracle, Balaam is suddenly and strangely moved to think of his own death:

> Let me die the death of the righteous,
>> and let my end be like his! (Num 23:10)

Down below in the valley the people of Israel are peacefully encamped, totally unaware of the danger that threatens them. This is a picture of the way in which God's conflict against the powers of the demonic curse is carried on—outside the range of human powers and of anything that people can do. The people on earth who seem to be most intimately concerned are just doing nothing. Balak is no more than a spectator to what Balaam is doing; and Israel is calmly encamped in the valley without anxiety. The only powers engaged are those that lie above the level of the play of human forces. On one side is Balaam, who has the power to set in motion the forces of the underworld (or rather, who has himself fallen under the power of those forces of the underworld); on the other side is God the Lord. Once again we emphasize that this is exactly what the narrator wants to make plain; the decision in this conflict is not in the hands of men, it belongs to a higher dimension than the human. In earlier times, people would have said quite plainly that this is a conflict between God and the devil.

In the succeeding oracles of blessing, the vision of the seer stretches out to ever-wider horizons. God cannot lie! A word spoken by him can never fall to the ground (Num 23:19). It is only on the basis of this simple conviction that we can explain how the expectation of a future salvation and judgment grew in Israel to so mighty a stream. In every period prophets arose in Israel and foretold the future; and that which remained unfulfilled in the present must be maintained through all the generations as expectation, until it shall please God to glorify himself in the fulfillment. No promise of God can remain forever unfulfilled.

There is some reason to think that there existed in Israel a kind of Enthronement Festival, a solemn ceremony in which the coming of God and of his kingdom were celebrated in a great act of worship.[10] The people of the old covenant saw that in the world there is still much which resists the sovereignty of God. For that reason it lived always in a state of eager expectation of the time of the decisive triumph of God, of the time when God will be accepted as king throughout all the earth. The climax of this festival was probably a great shout of triumph at the thought of this manifestation of the sovereignty of God that is so soon to come. It is something like this rousing cry of triumph that now suddenly strikes upon the ear of the alien diviner, which God has opened to hear his word. And now he understands the truth: If a people waits in such readiness for the coming of the kingdom of God, against that people no magic or sorcery can prevail (Num 23:21).

10. [Ed.] On the Enthronement Festival in ancient Israel and related psalms, see von Rad, *Old Testament Theology*, vol. 1, 362–64; and Mowinckel, *The Psalms in Israel's Worship*, vol. 1, 106–92.

Balak is furious at all this; but his fury cannot check the stream of blessing that flows from Balaam's mouth. In his third oracle, Balaam pours forth a tremendous song in praise of the promised land:

> How fair are your tents, O Jacob,
>> your encampments, O Israel!
> Like palm-groves that stretch far away,
>> like gardens beside a river,
> like aloes that Yahweh has planted,
>> like cedar trees beside the waters. (Num 24:5–6)

This is the land that God has chosen, in order that he may lay there the foundation of his coming kingdom.

Now at last Balak's patience is at an end. He decides to drive Balaam away. Balaam breaks off his stream of prophecy. But, just as he is about to take his departure, completely unbidden he falls again into prophetic utterance. His spirit presses forward to the furthest goal of the history of salvation as it is revealed in the Old Testament. At this point the spirit of the seer is reaching out and touching what really is the end of all things. This is made plain by the circumstantial and especially solemn introduction to his speech:

> So he uttered his oracle, saying,
> "The oracle of Balaam the son of Beor,
>> the oracle of the man whose eye is clear,
> the oracle of one who hears the words of God,
>> and knows the knowledge of the Most High,
> who sees the vision of the Almighty,
>> who falls down, but with his eyes uncovered."
> (Num 24:15–16)

It looks as though the seer was afraid to give up this last secret, or at least to make it too easily available to the understanding of the hearers. For this reason, he makes them share with him the laborious concentration, the suppression, the elimination, of all individual mental life that are needed if a person is to be the vehicle of such an ultimate divine revelation. The eyes of his body are closed; only in this way can he receive the revelation of the Almighty. "Falling down"—he can receive it only in the attitude of the most complete humility before God. And then he lets us see how, when a person has thus renounced one's self in meditation, the outlines of the distant vision gradually begin to become plain. Not all at once but gradually the principal features of that most distant and most mysterious revelation begin to be discerned:

> I see him, but not now;
>> I behold him, but not near:
> a star shall come forth out of Jacob,
>> and a scepter shall rise out of Israel.
> (Num 24:17)

The Messiah! Here Balaam touches on that expectation of a ruler, sent by God to deliver, of which we find so many evidences in the Old Testament. But the prophets do not all depict the figure of this messianic king in the same way. In Isaiah we find the picture of a Messiah who establishes the righteousness of God upon earth and is a helper of the poor (Isa 11:1–5). In Genesis 49:9–12, we find one

> Binding his foal to the vine
>> and his donkey's colt to the choice vine,

> he washes his garments in wine
>> and his robe in the blood of grapes;
> his eyes are darker than wine,
>> and his teeth whiter than milk.
>
> (Gen 49:11–12)

Are we back in the garden of Eden? Is this the restoration of the original blessing pronounced by God upon humans?[11]

As Christians we are bound to say that in each one of these pictures there is something of Christ; but each of them is linked to the ideas of a particular time, and these ideas are not in themselves of permanent significance. Balaam says of the Messiah that he "shall crush the borderlands of Moab" (Num 24:17). This makes it clear that the full picture of the Christ as we know him in the New Testament has not dawned on his vision. Moab and Balak—these are for him types of the powers that are hostile to God, and set themselves in array against that realm that God has chosen for his own and has taken under his own protection. And these are the hostile powers—so the oracle of Balaam foretells—that the anointed of the Lord shall vanquish in the end.

From this climax the story falls steeply away to its conclusion. Balak gives up his attempt to injure Israel, and Balaam goes back to his own home (Num 24:25).

This whole story of Balaam is not a tale told without a purpose. In the form in which we now have it, it is the expression of certain quite definite beliefs, of the central doctrines of the Old Testament revelation. God stands alongside his own people to help them. They do not depend upon humans or upon power politics for their protection.

---

11. [Ed.] On this passage, see von Rad, *Genesis*, 424–26.

Furthermore, even the most sinister purposes of the enemy against God's people are bound to be transformed in such a way as to benefit them. Balaam comes to curse—but he stays to bless. Thus the story makes visibly plain to us something that otherwise we should be able to grasp only by a daring and adventurous faith. All history has a secret inner side, which is hidden from the eyes of the natural person. The story of Balaam turns history inside out and makes the miracle plain. Balaam comes desiring to curse; and, as we may say, in the very teeth of his desires the curse is turned into a blessing.

Now, if we call this "a tale," we must not use the term in the sense of a story of wish-fulfillment, dictated by nothing but the human imagination; it corresponds to a reality that the people of the old covenant had experienced and tested in a long history of fellowship with their God. The Christian Church, looking back on its own history, must confess that it too has often been heir to the blessing of Balaam. This story also sets forth in visible form the truth of the New Testament saying: "We know that all things work together for good for those who love God, who are called according to his purpose" (Rom 8:28).

Conclusion

In the last book of the Bible we read of those who sing "the song of Moses, the servant of God, and the song of the Lamb" (Rev 15:3). It began in Moses; it is fulfilled in Christ. We have tried to set out briefly the main lines of the revelation of God as it came to Moses. What are these lines? There is, first, the calling of a people chosen by God to live directly under his guidance and in obedience to his will. This is a calling to pilgrimage, to movement in the direction of a promised land. There is the revelation of a God who dwells in the midst of his people in mercy and in judgment. There is the communication of a law of God, which is given as a guardian and a guide, and which is to be accepted and observed with joy. There is the vision of an expanding purpose to be fulfilled at the end of the ages, when all nations will be brought into the kingdom of God.

If the readers of this book have some acquaintance with the New Testament, they will have no difficulty in recognizing that all these principles of the Old Testament revelation are still in full force, though in modified forms, in the New. What was dimly shown in Moses has been shown to us very much more clearly in Jesus Christ. And, just because we have so much fuller light, the responsibility that rests on us is heavier than that which rested on the people of God in the Old Testament.

Bibliography

Barton, John. "'The Work of Human Hands' (Psalm 115:4): Idolatry in the Old Testament." In *The Ten Commandments: The Reciprocity of Faithfulness*, edited by William P. Brown, 144–203. Library of Theological Ethics. Louisville: Westminster John Knox, 2004.

Brueggemann, Walter. *A Commentary on Jeremiah: Exile and Homecoming*. Grand Rapids: Eerdmans, 1998.

———. *Genesis*. Interpretation. Atlanta: John Knox, 1982.

———. *Hopeful Imagination: Prophetic Voices in Exile*. Philadelphia: Fortress, 1986.

———. *The Land: Place as Gift, Promise, and Challenge in Biblical Faith*. 2nd ed. Overtures to Biblical Theology. Minneapolis: Fortress, 2002.

Capetz, Paul E. "The First Commandment as a Theological and Ethical Principle." In *The Ten Commandments: The Reciprocity of Faithfulness*, edited by William P. Brown, 174–92. Library of Theological Ethics. Louisville: Westminster John Knox, 2004.

Childs, Brevard S. *The Book of Exodus: A Critical, Theological Commentary*. Old Testament Library. Philadelphia: Westminster, 1974.

Coats, George W. "Balaam: Saint or Sinner?" In *Saga, Legend, Tale, Novella, Fable: Narrative Forms in Old Testament Literature*, edited by George W. Coats, 56–62. Journal for the Study of the Old Testament Supplement Series 35. Sheffield, UK: JSOT Press, 1985.

———. *Moses: Heroic Man of God*. Journal for the Study of the Old Testament Supplement Series 57. Sheffield, UK: JSOT Press, 1988.

———. "The Moses Narratives as Heroic Saga." In *Saga, Legend, Tale, Novella, Fable: Narrative Forms in Old Testament Literature*, edited by George W. Coats, 33–44. Journal for the Study of the Old Testament Supplement Series 35. Sheffield, UK: JSOT Press, 1985.

Freedman, David Noel, M. P. O'Connor, and Helmer Ringgren. "יהוה YHWH." In *Theological Dictionary of the Old Testament*, edited by G. Johannes Botterweck and Helmer Rinngren, 5:500–521. Grand Rapids: Eerdmans, 1986.

Habel, Norman. *The Land Is Mine: Six Biblical Land Ideologies*. Overtures to Biblical Theology. Philadelphia: Fortress, 1995.

Hackett, Jo Ann. "Balaam." In *The Anchor Bible Dictionary*, edited by David Noel Freedman, 1:569–72. New York: Doubleday, 1992.

Mowinckel, Sigmund. *The Psalms in Israel's Worship*. 2 vols. in 1. Translated by D. R. Ap-Thomas. 1962. Reprinted with a new Foreword by James L. Crenshaw. Biblical Resource Series. Grand Rapids: Eerdmans, 2004.

Olson, Dennis T. *Deuteronomy and the Death of Moses: A Theological Reading*. Overtures to Biblical Theology. Minneapolis: Fortress, 1994.

Rad, Gerhard von. *Deuteronomy: A Commentary*. Translated by Dorothea Barton. Old Testament Library. Philadelphia: Westminster, 1966.

———. *From Genesis to Chronicles: Explorations in Old Testament Theology*. Translated by E. W. T. Dicken. Edited by K. C. Hanson. Fortress Classics in Biblical Studies. Minneapolis: Fortress, 2005.

———. *Old Testament Theology*. 2 vols. Translated by D. M. G. Stalker. 1966, 1970. Reprinted with new Introduction by Walter Brueggemann. Old Testament Library. Louisville: Westminster John Knox, 2001.

———. "The Story of Balaam." In *God at Work in Israel*, 36–39. Translated by John H. Marks. Nashville: Abingdon, 1980.

———. "Typological Interpretation of the Old Testament." In *Essays on Old Testament Hermeneutics*, edited by Claus Westermann, 17–39. Richmond, VA: John Knox, 1963.

Richardson, M. E. J. *Hammurabi's Laws: Text, Translation, and Glossary*. Biblical Seminar 73. Sheffield, UK: Sheffield Academic, 2000.

Roth, Martha. "The Laws of Hammurabi." In *The Context of Scripture*, vol. 2, *Monumental Inscriptions*, edited by William W. Hallo et al., 335–53. Leiden: Brill, 2000.

Westermann, Claus. *Genesis 12–36*. Translated by John J. Scullion. Continental Commentaries. Minneapolis: Augsburg, 1985.

Further Reading

MOSES

Blenkinsopp, Joseph. *The Pentateuch: An Introduction to the First Five Books of the Bible*. Anchor Bible Reference Library. New York: Doubleday, 1992.

Britt, Brian. *Rewriting Moses: The Narrative Eclipse of the Text*. Journal for the Study of the Old Testament Supplement Series 402. London: T. & T. Clark, 2004.

Brueggemann, Walter. "The Alternative Community of Moses." In *The Prophetic Imagination*, 1–19. 2nd ed. Minneapolis: Fortress, 2001.

Buber, Martin. *Moses: The Revelation and the Covenant*. New York: Harper, 1958.

Coats, George W. *Moses: Heroic Man of God*. Journal for the Study of the Old Testament Supplement Series 57. Sheffield, UK: JSOT Press, 1988.

———. *The Moses Tradition*. Journal for the Study of the Old Testament Supplement Series 161. Sheffield, UK: JSOT Press, 1993.

———, editor. *Saga, Legend, Tale, Novella, Fable: Narrative Forms in Old Testament Literature*. Journal for the Study of the Old Testament Supplement Series 35. Sheffield, UK: JSOT Press, 1985.

Gottwald, Norman K. "Traditions about Moses: Exodus, Covenant, and Lawgiving." In *The Hebrew Bible: A Socio-Literary Introduction*, 179–227. Philadelphia: Fortress, 1985.

~

The Ten Commandments and the Law

Braaten, Carl E. *I Am the Lord Your God: Christian Reflections on the Ten Commandments*. Grand Rapids: Eerdmans, 2005.

Brown, William P., editor. *The Ten Commandments: The Reciprocity of Faithfulness*. Library of Theological Ethics. Louisville: Westminster John Knox, 2004.

Chittister, Joan. *The Ten Commandments: Laws of the Heart*. Maryknoll, NY: Orbis, 2006.

Crüsemann, Frank. *The Torah: Theology and Social History of Old Testament Law*. Translated by Allan W. Mahnke. Minneapolis: Fortress, 1996.

Harrelson, Walter J. *The Ten Commandments and Human Rights*. Overtures to Biblical Theology. Philadelphia: Fortress, 1980.

———. *The Ten Commandments for Today*. Louisville: Westminster John Knox, 2006.

Hauerwas, Stanley, and William H. Willimon. *The Truth about God: The Ten Commandments in Christian Life*. Nashville: Abingdon, 1999.

Miller, Patrick D. *The Ten Commandments*. Interpretation. Louisville: Westminster John Knox, 2009.

Patrick, Dale. *Old Testament Law*. Atlanta: John Knox, 1985.

Zimmerli, Walther. *The Law and the Prophets: A Study in the Meaning of the Old Testament*. Translated by R. E. Clements. Oxford: Blackwell, 1965.

∽

Additional Works by Gerhard von Rad

Biblical Interpretations in Preaching. Translated by John E. Steely. Nashville: Abingdon, 1977.

Genesis: A Commentary. Translated by John H. Marks. Rev. ed. Old Testament Library. Philadelphia: Westminster, 1972.

God at Work in Israel. Translated by John H. Marks. Nashville: Abingdon, 1980.

Further Reading

Holy War in Ancient Israel. Translated and edited by Marva J. Dawn. 1991. Reprint, Eugene, OR: Wipf & Stock, 2000.

Studies in Deuteronomy. Translated by David Stalker. Studies in Biblical Theology 1/9. Chicago: Regnery, 1953.

Wisdom in Israel. Translated by James D. Martin. Nashville: Abingdon, 1972.

Scripture Index

OLD TESTAMENT

Genesis

2:21	24
12:2–3	69
12:3	81
15:12	24
32:22–32	21
32:29–30	22
49:9–12	84
49:11–12	85

Exodus

2:11–12	15
3:1–3	16
3:7–14	16–19
5:20–21	8
14:11–12	8
14:11	9
16	72
16:2–3	8
16:16	72
17:2–3	8
20	55
20:2–3	29
20:4	38
20:7a	24–25
21–23	45
21:12–17	49
22:1–15	46
22:25	53
22:26–27	52–53
23:1–9	51–52
24:15–18	9–10
32	40
32:1	5, 40
32:3	40
32:4	41
32:6	42
32:17–20	42
32:21	42
32:23–24	42
32:23	5
32:25	42
33:7–11	11
33:18–23	23
33:19	23
34:29–35	10

Leviticus

17–26	45
19:2	51
19:12	25
19:17–18	54
19:18	62
21:1	31
25:2–4	56
25:23	56

Numbers

5:2	31
9:10	31
11:1–6	8
11:10–15	7
11:24–30	7
11:29	9
12:1–2	8
12:3	5
13–14	73
13:27	74
13:31	8
14:1–4	8
14:3	9, 75
14:4	74
14:7	74
14:8–9	74
14:10–11	74
14:21	75
14:31	75
14:44–45	75
16	9
16:1–3	8
16:5	9
19:14–16	31
20:1–5	8
21:5	8

22–24	76
22:6	77
22:9–21	78
22:20	78
22:22	77
22:35	78
23:8	80
23:9	80
23:10	81
23:19	82
23:21	82
24:5–6	83
24:15–16	83
24:17	84
24:25	85

Deuteronomy

1:34–37	11
3:24–25	12
3:26	12
4:21–24	11
6:5	62
8:2–3	73
9:7–21	11
9:25–29	11
12–26	45
15:1–2	58
15:9–10	59
17	48
17:8–11	48
18	31
18:9–12	31
18:13	35
18:15	32
24:10–11	53
24:14–15	53
27	49

27:15–26	59–60
27:15	43
29:29	32–33
30:11–14	33–35
30:15–19	64
32:46–47	64
33:1	8
34	12
34:7	12

Joshua

1:1	8
14:6	8
24:14–15	36

Judges

13	19–21
13:11	20
13:15	20
13:17	20
13:18	20

1 Kings

8:61	35
11:4	35
15:3	35
15:14	35
18:21	36

Psalms

19:1	39
19:7–13	63
23:3	22–23
24	62
24:1	62
119	63

Isaiah

7:4	37
11:1–5	84
22:8–11	37
30:15	37
40–55	69
49:14–21	70
52:7–12	70
54	70

Jeremiah

2:6	71
23:23	25
26:10	46
31:31–34	66

Ezekiel

36:26–27	66

Hosea

13:5	71

❧

NEW TESTAMENT

Mark

12:29	62

Luke

4:16–21	26
4:21	26
24:27	26

Scripture Index

John

5:39	26
6:15	27

Acts

2	9

Romans

8:28	86
8:29	67

1 Corinthians

10:11	72

2 Corinthians

12:9	24

Colossians

3:3	67

Hebrews

7:26	14
8:5	71

Revelation

15:3	86

Lightning Source UK Ltd.
Milton Keynes UK
UKHW041506230322
400499UK00003B/825